Research-Based Strategies

Narrowing the Achievement Gap for Under-Resourced Students

Research-Based Strategies: Narrowing the Achievement Gap for
   Under-Resourced Students
© 2009 by aha! Process, Inc. Revised 2010.
   Ruby K. Payne
      300 pp.
      Bibliography pp. 265–300

aha! Process, Inc.
P.O. Box 727
Highlands, TX 77562-0727
(800) 424-9484 ▪ (281) 426-5300
Fax: (281) 426-5600
Website: www.ahaprocess.com

Library of Congress Control Number: 2009929502

   ISBN 13: 978-1-934583-34-0

Copy editing by Dan Shenk and Jesse Conrad
Book design by Paula Nicolella
Cover design by Naylor Design

Printed in the United States of America

Research-Based Strategies

Narrowing the Achievement Gap
for Under-Resourced Students

Ruby K. Payne, Ph.D.

ACKNOWLEDGMENTS

I would like to thank:

- Peggy Black, for her suggestions around organization of the strategies and observed behaviors.

- Dr. Cheryl Sattler, for her research assistance.

- Dr. Donna Magee, for her careful reading and organizational recommendations.

- Peggy Conrad, for her work to get this book published.

- All aha! Process consultants for their valuable feedback and suggestions.

TABLE OF CONTENTS

* This strategy has been repeated because of its significance to working
  with under-resourced learners. It has Applications in this area, as
  well as where it was first introduced on p. 109.

FOREWORD

Those familiar with the work of aha! Process, Inc. and Dr. Ruby Payne realize that the practitioner is at the heart of the work. Providing research-based strategies that can be readily implemented and integrated into any curriculum or program that will raise student achievement has always been the focus of efforts by aha! Process. In this redesign of the original *Learning Structures,* you will find a "menu" of strategies that can be used to meet the needs of today's under-resourced learners. These strategies are not a prescription of services; rather, they are designed for you to implement after you have completed an analysis of your students' needs. Whether you base this analysis on state assessment results, formative assessments, daily observation, or classwork doesn't matter. The important thing is that you are monitoring students' progress and promptly making interventions as needed. Interventions made after a student has failed typically result in a student falling farther behind, often not being able to recover—and sometimes even dropping out of school as a result.

You will note that we have incorporated the book *Understanding Learning: the How, the Why, the What.* This is provided so that you have a basic understanding of learning theory that supports these interventions. In keeping with the premise that all learning is about the *what,* the *why,* and the *how,* the interventions are then formatted in this same way—providing you the *what* (the strategy), the *why* (the need for the particular strategy), and the *how* (explanation or process). The research base for each also is provided. To facilitate your addressing the needs of your students more readily, the strategies have been grouped according to academics, behavior, academics and behavior together, and communitywide strategies that we are finding are needed to build community sustainability.

When working with these strategies, several tips should be considered. First, flexibility in their use is key; if you try the strategy and it doesn't work, reflect upon why it didn't work. Modify it and try again. If that doesn't work, then perhaps it isn't appropriate for the student, and you might want to try something else. Second, at a time when our classrooms are more diverse than ever, differentiation is an absolute necessity. This menu of strategies can assist you in differentiating for your students. Third, use the strategies to meet the mandates of Response to Intervention. As the educator, you have incredible influence upon the success of your students; but we must make interventions simpler to use, yet they must have high impact and give a payoff for our time.

Finally, if you are familiar with the *Learning Structures,* you will note that we have included a number of the same strategies that appeared in that workbook. We have done this because our research, as well as your feedback, has indicated that they work. Just because something is not new does not mean it lacks value. So as you flip through these pages and start working with these interventions, feel free to adapt and modify them. Make them work for you. We hope you will find the additional strategies—and this reformatting that offers greater flexibility in use—to be beneficial.

–Donna Magee, Ed.D.

PURPOSE OF BOOK AND HOW TO USE IT

PURPOSE OF THE BOOK

The purpose of this book is to provide strategies for teachers so that they can narrow/eliminate the achievement gap for under-resourced students. Does the following chart (on Academic Strategies, Researchers, and Explanation) have all the answers? No. But it does provide many tools to begin the process of increasing achievement.

Historically, we have taken resourced students and put them into a box called school, and they come out more resourced. When under-resourced students came into school, many times they dropped out or failed because the resources/supports were not there for them. Our task now is to have under-resourced students enter this box called school and also come out more resourced.

HOW TO USE THIS BOOK

The book is organized this way:

1 The first chart is called OBSERVED BEHAVIORS AND STRATEGY NUMBERS. When you observe a behavior, next to the behavior is a strategy number.

2 When you know the strategy number, you use the second chart. The second chart is called RESEARCH-BASED STRATEGIES TO USE WITH UNDER-RESOURCED LEARNERS. This chart identifies what the strategy is, the researchers, a short explanation, and then the page number in this book where there is further explanation and an example.

3 Go to that page number, read the explanation and see the example, and use them with the student. These strategies can also be used as a part of the RTI (Response to Intervention) process.

4 In the Appendixes is the transcript of a book called *Understanding Learning*. This is a quick read for a better understanding of what a student must do inside his/her head in order to learn.

I wish you wonderful success. It is going to take everyone working together to eliminate the achievement gap, which must not be allowed to continue to exist simply because a student does not have resources. We can do this.

OBSERVED BEHAVIORS AND STRATEGY NUMBERS

WITH OTHER PEOPLE

OBSERVED BEHAVIOR	STRATEGY NUMBER TO USE
Does not work well with others	33, 34, 38, 39, 43, 44, 46, 47, 50
Bullies others	33, 34, 36, 38, 40, 41, 43
Socializes excessively	14, 33, 34, 37, 40, 41
Has almost no friends; isolated	18, 19, 32, 33, 43, 44, 46
Has few words to resolve conflicts	16, 37, 38, 39, 40

WITH TASKS/ASSIGNMENTS

OBSERVED BEHAVIOR	STRATEGY NUMBER TO USE
Does assignment incorrectly	2, 3, 5, 6, 7, 8, 11, 12, 17, 20, 21, 22, 23, 30
Does not hand in work done outside of class	1, 14, 18, 33, 34, 37, 39, 45, 50
Cannot transfer information from board to paper	26, 28
Does not hand in work done in class	8, 14, 33, 34, 45
Does not follow directions	5, 8, 30
Will not attempt task	3, 6, 7, 8, 19, 30, 33, 34, 35, 45
Misuses time	5, 8, 14, 15, 30, 33, 41, 45
Skips steps/parts of assignment	5, 6, 7, 8, 12, 30

WITH CONTENT

OBSERVED BEHAVIOR	STRATEGY NUMBER TO USE
Overwhelmed by information presented	2, 3, 8, 11
Not on grade level	1, 4, 51
Does not know purpose of content	2, 3
Does not remember information next day	3, 21, 25, 31

WITH MANAGING SELF/BEHAVIOR

OBSERVED BEHAVIOR	STRATEGY NUMBER TO USE
Does not follow school rules	33, 38, 39, 40, 41, 43, 50
Interrupts teacher/class	33, 34, 39, 40, 42, 43
Entertains rather than does work	32, 33, 34
Sleeps in class	32, 47, 53
Disengaged, not motivated	13, 32, 36, 44, 46, 47, 48, 49, 53
Has difficulty focusing	25, 48
Health issues interfere with learning	32, 57

WITH READING/WRITING/LANGUAGE

OBSERVED BEHAVIOR	STRATEGY NUMBER TO USE
Cannot discern what is and is not important to remember in text	6, 21, 22
Writing samples are disorganized	3, 12, 17, 29
Writing samples are short, with limited vocabulary	9, 16, 17, 24, 27, 29
Writes below grade level	1, 3, 9, 29
Does not complete constructed response questions on tests	4, 8, 20, 30
Uses inappropriate verb tenses in writing	24, 29
Cannot discriminate main idea	6, 21, 22, 30
Unwilling to read	10, 18, 19, 30
Cannot decode with fluency	10, 31
Can read but does not understand what was read	4, 6, 21, 22
Has mostly casual register vocabulary	4, 9, 16, 24

WITH MATH

OBSERVED BEHAVIOR	STRATEGY NUMBER TO USE
Has difficulty with problem solving	5, 7, 8
Cannot follow columns and rows	26, 27
Cannot follow most math processes	7, 8, 30
Does not know math facts in multiplication, addition, subtraction	31
Has difficulty with math vocabulary	9, 16, 20, 24, 30
Has difficulty with math concepts	2, 3, 16, 42
Cannot rotate visual figures (geometry)	26, 42
Has difficulty doing equations	20, 25, 26

WITH EXTERNAL RESOURCE SUPPORTS

OBSERVED BEHAVIOR	STRATEGY NUMBER TO USE
Has frequent unexcused absences	32, 47, 53, 57
Has excessive tardies	32, 47, 53, 57

RESEARCH-BASED STRATEGIES TO USE
WITH UNDER-RESOURCED LEARNERS

STRATEGY NUMBER	PAGE NUMBER	ACADEMIC STRATEGIES	RESEARCHERS	EXPLANATION
1	53	Extra time—using technology, scheduling (double periods), or tutors	Bloom, B. (1976). TIME/SCHEDULING: Farbman, D., and Kaplan, C. (2005). Farmer-Hinton, R. L. (2002). Gladwell, M. (2008). Mattox, K., Hancock, D., and Queen, J. A. (2005). TECHNOLOGY: Behrmann, M., and Jerome, M. K. (2002). Swan, K., van Hooft, M., Kratcoski, A., and Unger, D. (2005). Williams, A., Rouse, K., Seals, C., and Gilbert, J. (2009). Wright, J.C., and Huston, A. C. (1995). OTHER: "Report of the National Education Commission on Time and Learning." (1994). Rocha, E. (2008).	Extra time is one of four variables that impact student learning. Using flip video cameras, lessons can be recorded and burned to DVD or stored on a portable device like a laptop or iPod video to be visited again by students. Double periods back to back to increase learning time. Tutors may also be used to provide extra learning time.

STRATEGY NUMBER	PAGE NUMBER	ACADEMIC STRATEGIES	RESEARCHERS	EXPLANATION
2	54	Content comprehension (structure, purpose, pattern, process of the discipline)	Bransford, J. D., Brown, A. L., and Cocking, R. R. (Eds.). (2000). Donovan, M. S., and Bransford, J. D. (2005). Hill, H. C., Blunk, M. L., Charalambous, Y., Lewis, J. M., Phelps, G. C., Sleep, L., and Ball, D. L. (2008). Kilpatrick, J., Swafford, J., and Findell, B. (Eds.). (2001). Krauss, S., Brunner, M., Kunter, M., Baumert, J., Neubrand, M., Blum, W., et al. (2008). Senge, P. (1994). Shulman, L. (1987).	All content has a purpose, as well as structures, patterns, and processes. That is the basis for determining what is and is not important in the discipline. These can be represented by concept maps, mental models, and visual representations.

STRATEGY NUMBER	PAGE NUMBER	ACADEMIC STRATEGIES	RESEARCHERS	EXPLANATION
3	56	Mental models for academic content	Baghban, M. (2007). Bailey, M., et al. (1995). Donovan, M. S., and Bransford, J. D. (2005). Guastello, E. F., Beasley, T. M., and Sinatra, R. C., (2000). Herman, T., Colton, S., and Franzen, M. (2008). Idol, L., and Jones, B.F. (1991). Jones, B. F., Pierce, J., Hunter, B. (1988). Kilpatrick, J., Swafford, J., and Findell, B. (Eds.). (2001). Lin, H., and Chen, T. (2006). Marzano, R. (2007). Marzano, R., and Arrendondo, D. (1986). McCrudden, M. T., Schraw, G., and Lehman, S. (2009). Payne, R. K. (2005). Payne, R. K. (2007). Resnick, L., and Klopfer, L. (1989). Schnotz, W., and Kurschner, C. (2008). Senge, P. (1994). Shulman, L. (1987).	Mental models are drawings, stories, and analogies that translate ideas into sensory representations or experiences that help make sense of information and increase memory of information.

STRATEGY NUMBER	PAGE NUMBER	ACADEMIC STRATEGIES	RESEARCHERS	EXPLANATION
4	64	Composing questions	Campbell, T. (2006). Chin, C., and Kayalvizhi, G. (2002). Chin, C., and Osborne, J. (2008). del Mar Badia Martin, M., Gotzens Busquet, C., Genovard Rossello, C., and Castelló Tarrida, A. (2007). Dermody, M. M., Speaker, R. B., Jr. (1999). McManus, D. O., Dunn, R., and Denig, S. J. (2003). National Institute of Child Health and Human Development. (2000). Palincsar, A., and Brown, A. L. (1984). Parker, M., and Hurry, J. (2007). Walberg, H. (1990). Whalon, K., and Hanline, M. F. (2008).	If students say, "I don't understand," and you ask what part don't they understand, and they say, "All of it," or "None of it," they probably cannot ask a question syntactically. Palincsar correlated it with reading achievement. Walberg gave it an effect size of .35— i.e., test scores are one third higher on average.

STRATEGY NUMBER	PAGE NUMBER	ACADEMIC STRATEGIES	RESEARCHERS	EXPLANATION
5	75	Procedural self-talk	Callicott, K. J., and Park, H. (2003). Fernyhough, C., and Fradley, E. (2005). Feuerstein, R. (1980). Kishiyama, M. M., Boyce, W. T., Jimenez, A. M., Perry L. M., and Knight, R. T. (2008). Manfra, L., and Winsler, A. (2006). Ostad, S. A., and Askeland, M. (2008). Stamou, E., Theodorakis, Y., Kokaridas, D., Perkos, S., and Kessanopoulou, M. (2007).	To complete tasks involves prefrontal activity—planning. Planning requires procedural self-talk. Because the executive functions of some poor children's brains are less developed, planning and self-talk can be directly taught using games and procedural tools.

STRATEGY NUMBER	PAGE NUMBER	ACADEMIC STRATEGIES	RESEARCHERS	EXPLANATION
6	76	Nonfiction reading strategy (input process)	Feuerstein, R. (1980). Gaddy, S. A., Bakken, J. P., and Fulk, B. M. (2008). Gajria, M., Jitendra, A. K., Sood, S., and Sacks, G. (2007). Hall, K. M., Sabey, B. L., and McClellan, M. (2005). McCrudden, M. T., Schraw, G., and Lehman, S. (2009). Montelongo, J., Berber-Jimenez, L., Hernandez, A. C., and Hosking, D. (2006). National Institute of Child Health and Human Development. (2000). Rogevich, M. E., and Perin, D. (2008). van den Bos, K. P., Nakken, H., Nicolay, P. G., and van Houten, E. J. (2007). Williams, J. P., Hall, K. M., Lauer, K. D., Stafford, K. B., DeSisto, L. A., and deCani, J. S. (2005). Williams, J. P., Stafford, K. B., Lauer, K. D., Hall, K. M., and Pollini, S. (2009).	To complete a task requires a systematic approach.

STRATEGY NUMBER	PAGE NUMBER	ACADEMIC STRATEGIES	RESEARCHERS	EXPLANATION
7	82	Problem-solving process (input process)	Boulware-Gooden, R., Carreker, S., Thornhill, A., and Joshi, R. M. (2007). Feuerstein, R. (1980). Fuchs, L. S., Fuchs, D., Prentice, K., Hamlett, C. L., Finelli, R., and Courey, S. J. (2004). Morrison, J. A., and Young, T. A., (2008). Schraw, G., Brooks, D., and Crippen, K. J. (2005). Singh, C. (2008). Star, J. R., and Rittle-Johnson, B. (2008).	To complete a task requires a systematic approach.
8	84	Step sheets (input process)	Beatham, M. D. (2009). Feuerstein, R. (1980). Krueger, K. A., and Dayan, P. (2009). Lodewyk, K. R., Winne, P. H., and Jamieson-Noel, D. L. (2009). Marzano, R., and Arrendondo, D. (1986). Ngu, B. H., Mit, E., Shahbodin, F., and Tuovinen, J. (2009).	To complete tasks requires planning, which requires procedural self-talk. Because the executive functions of some poor children's brains are less developed, planning and self-talk can be directly taught using games and procedural tools.

STRATEGY NUMBER	PAGE NUMBER	ACADEMIC STRATEGIES	RESEARCHERS	EXPLANATION
9	87	Sketching for vocabulary	Apperly, I. A., Williams, E., and Williams, J. (2004). Marzano, R. (2007). Paquette, K. R., Fello, S. E., and Jalongo, M. R. (2007). Rohrer, T. (2006). Tanenhaus, M. K., Spivey-Knowlton, M. J., Eberhard, K. M., and Sedivy, J. C. (1995). Van Meter, P., Aleksic, M., Schwartz, A., and Garner, J. (2006).	Visual memory precedes verbal memory. Linguistic definitions were preceded by a visual representation in the brain.

STRATEGY NUMBER	PAGE NUMBER	ACADEMIC STRATEGIES	RESEARCHERS	EXPLANATION
10	89	Tucker signing strategy for decoding	Cole, C., and Majd, M. (2005) Thompson, R. L., Vinson, D. P., and Vigliocco, G. (2009).	The Center on Education and Lifelong Learning at Indiana University, in its evaluation of this decoding strategy, found the following growth: With the progress score being the difference between the number of words students could read on the pre- and post-tests, the mean progress score for the control group—no Tucker reading instruction—was only 5.30 points, as compared with 36.75 points for the experimental group. A student must be able to decode in order to comprehend. Decoding means that you know a symbol, e.g., *sh* represents a sound. This is a kinesthetic approach that uses both sides of the brain.

STRATEGY NUMBER	PAGE NUMBER	ACADEMIC STRATEGIES	RESEARCHERS	EXPLANATION
11	91	Taking control of your own learning tools	Brink, J., Capps, E., and Sutko, A. (2004). Gladwell, M. (2008). Hoffman, A. (2003). Kirby, N. F., and Downs, C. T. (2007). Po-ying, C. (2007). Thompson, D. D., and McDonald, D. M. (2007).	Complexity, autonomy, and the relationship between effort and reward are the prerequisites for making meaning (Gladwell, 2008).
12	93	Self-assessment rubrics	Andrade, H. G. (1999a). Andrade, H. G. (1999b). Andrade, H. L., Du, Y., and Wang, X. (2008). Bloom, B. (1976). Bransford, J. D., Brown, A. L., and Cocking, R. R. (Eds.). (2000). Goddard, Y. L., and Sendi, C. (2008). Hafner, J. C., and Hafner, P. M. (2003). National Institute of Child Health and Human Development. (2000). Ross, J. A., and Starling, M. (2008).	Evaluation is at the highest level of Bloom's Taxonomy in thinking. It echoes Gladwell's comments above.

STRATEGY NUMBER	PAGE NUMBER	ACADEMIC STRATEGIES	RESEARCHERS	EXPLANATION
13	95	Teaching another student	"ClassWide Peer Tutoring." (2007). "Peer Tutoring and Response Groups." (2007). Brooks, R. (1991). Kamps, D. M., Greenwood, C., Arreaga-Mayer, C., Veerkamp, M. B., Utley, C., Tapia, Y., et al. (2008). Kourea, L., Cartledge, G., and Musti-Rao, S. (2007). Roscoe, R. D., and Chi, M. T. H. (2008). Veerkamp, M. B., Kamps, D. M., and Cooper, L. (2007).	Brooks found that teaching another student yielded returns in achievement and resiliency.
14	96	Planning academic tasks	Bakunas, B., and Holley, W. (2004). Bransford, J. D., Brown, A. L., and Cocking, R. R. (Eds.). (2000). Chalmers, D., and Lawrence, J. A. (1993). Collier, P. J., and Morgan, D. L. (2008). Feuerstein, R. (1980). Gambill, J. M., Moss, L. A., and Vescogni, C. D. (2008). Garcia-Ros, R., Perez-Gonzalez, F., and Hinojosa, E. (2004). Stoeger, H., and Ziegler, A. (2008). Yumusak, N., Sungur, S., and Cakiroglu, J. (2007).	To complete tasks requires planning, which requires procedural self-talk. Because the executive functions of some poor children's brains are less developed, planning and self-talk can be directly taught using games and procedural tools.

STRATEGY NUMBER	PAGE NUMBER	ACADEMIC STRATEGIES	RESEARCHERS	EXPLANATION
15	98	Planning your grade	Feuerstein, R. (1980).	To complete tasks requires planning, which requires procedural self-talk. Because the executive functions of some poor children's brains are less developed, planning and self-talk can be directly taught using games and procedural tools.
16	101	Translating casual register to formal register	Adger, C. (1994). Godley, A. J., and Minnici, A. (2008). Koch, L. M., Gross, A. M., and Kolts, R. (2001). Montano-Harmon, M. R. (1991). Olmedo, I. M. (2009). Wheeler, R. S. (2008).	To build formal register, one must use the current vocabulary and build upon it. One way to build it is to translate casual register (what is known—current schema) to formal register.
17	102	Writing organizers/text patterns	Chalk, J. C., Hagan-Burke, S., and Burke, M. D. (2005). Guastello, E. F., Beasley, T. M., and Sinatra, R. C., (2000). Idol, L., and Jones, B. F. (Eds.). (1991). Lin, H., and Chen. T. (2006). Mason, L. H., and Shriner, J. G. (2008). National Institute of Child Health and Human Development. (2000). Williams, J. P. (2005). Williams, J. P., Hall, K. M., and Lauer, K. D. (2004).	To write, one must organize against purpose for writing and structure of text. Teaching text patterns and organizers facilitates this process.

STRATEGY NUMBER	PAGE NUMBER	ACADEMIC STRATEGIES	RESEARCHERS	EXPLANATION
18	109	Relational learning	Domagala-Zysk, E. (2006). Faircloth, B. S., and Hamm, J. V. (2005). Good, M., and Adams, G. R. (2008). Green, G., Rhodes, J., Hirsch, A. H., Suarez-Orozco, C., and Camic, P. M. (2008). Guay, F., Marsh, H. W., Senecal, C., and Dowson, M. (2008). Johnson, Lisa S. (2008). Payne, R. K. (2008). Putnam, R. (2000). Reis, S. M., Colbert, R. D., and Hebert, T. P. (2005). Rimm-Kaufman, S. E., and Chiu, Y.-J. I. (2007). Ross, D. D., Bondy, E., Gallingane, C., and Hambacher, E. (2008). Sanchez, B., Reyes, O., and Singh, J. (2006). Scales, P. C., Benson, P. L., Roehlkepartain, E. C., Sesma, A., Jr., and van Dulmen, M. (2006).	Relational learning involves seven characteristics. See Payne (2008).

STRATEGY NUMBER	PAGE NUMBER	ACADEMIC STRATEGIES	RESEARCHERS	EXPLANATION
19	111	Structured partners in learning	Bransford, J. D., Brown, A. L., and Cocking, R. R. (Eds.). (2000). Cheung, A., and Slavin, R. E. (2005). Galton, M., Hargreaves, L., and Pell, T. (2009). Gillies, R. M. (2004). Gillies, R. M. (2008). Mahalingam, M., Schaefer, F., and Morlino, E. (2008). National Institute of Child Health and Human Development. (2000).	Talking opens neural pathways, builds relationships, and enhances understandings.

STRATEGY NUMBER	PAGE NUMBER	ACADEMIC STRATEGIES	RESEARCHERS	EXPLANATION
20	112	Mental models for processes	Bransford, J. D., Brown, A. L., and Cocking, R. R. (Eds.). (2000). Bruner, J. (2006). Committee on the Support for Thinking Spatially. (2006). Idol, L., and Jones, B. F. (1991). Jones, B. F., Pierce, J., and Hunter, B. (1988). Marzano, R. (2007). Marzano, R., and Arrendondo, D. (1986). Payne, R. K. (2005 Payne, R. K. (2007). Resnick, L., and Klopfer, L. (1989). Senge, P. (1994). Shulman, L. (1987).	Visual representation is one of the areas in which poor and affluent brains are no different. Many studies indicate that mental models enhance learning. Bruner (2006) stated that all learning involves task and context.

STRATEGY NUMBER	PAGE NUMBER	ACADEMIC STRATEGIES	RESEARCHERS	EXPLANATION
21	115	Sorting important from unimportant using summarizing, cartooning, graphic organizers, visuals, compare/contrast activities	Guastello, E. F., Beasley, T. M., and Sinatra, R. C. (2000). Hagaman, J. L., and Reid, R. (2008). Hock, M., and Mellard, D. (2005). Kirkpatrick, L. C., and Klein, P. D. (2009). Langford, P. A., Rizzo, S. K., and Roth, J. M. (2003). Marzano, R. (2007). Reiner, M. (2009). Richards, J. C., and Anderson, N. A. (2003). Tanenhaus, M. K., Spivey-Knowlton, M. J., Eberhard, K. M., and Sedivy, J. C. (1995). van der Schoot, M., Vasbinder, A. L., Horsley, T. M., and van Lieshout, E. C. D. M. (2008). Weekes, H. (2005).	Memory is based upon summarization and/or attachment to prior knowledge. Summarization is based upon sorting important from unimportant. To sort what is and is not important, one must identify similarities and differences (compare and contrast).

STRATEGY NUMBER	PAGE NUMBER	ACADEMIC STRATEGIES	RESEARCHERS	EXPLANATION
22	121	Fiction reading organizer/sorter	Conlon, T. (2009). Idol, L., and Jones, B. F. (1991). Jones, B. F., Pierce, J., and Hunter, B. (1988). National Institute of Child Health and Human Development. (2000). Stone, R. H., Boon, R. T., Fore, C., III, Bender, W. N., and Spencer, V. G. (2008).	To summarize fiction, one has to remember the characters; the beginning, middle, and end (plot development); the setting; and the problem and/or goal. Any organizer that helps a student identify these things facilitates summarization and sorting.
23	126	Envelope system for research papers and reports	Ellis, K. D. (2004).	Models are necessary for the systematic gathering of data. The envelope system is for the facilitation of part to whole of tasks. Twenty percent of the grade is based upon using the process. Eighty percent of the grade is based on the final report.
24	128	Language/ vocabulary development	Carrell, C. (1987). Joshi, R. M. (2005). Tanenhaus, M. K., Spivey-Knowlton, M. J., Eberhard, K. M., and Sedivy, J. C. (1995).	Vocabulary is the tool the brain uses to think. Formal register is the vocabulary or ideas and abstract representational systems. Playful, relational, associative activities build vocabulary, as well as sketching.

STRATEGY NUMBER	PAGE NUMBER	ACADEMIC STRATEGIES	RESEARCHERS	EXPLANATION
25	136	Teaching input strategies using games	Gredler, M. E. (2004). Kishiyama, M. M., Boyce, W. T., Jimenez, A. M., Perry L. M., and Knight, R. T. (2008). Leemkuil, H., Jong, T. D., and Ootes, S. (2000). Rieber, L. P. (2005).	See attached charts on pages 138–139 of this book for games that can be used. Input strategies help one gather data. Games are relational and competitive, and they build many of these skills.
26	140	Spatial orientation/ transferring objects in representational space	Committee on the Support for Thinking Spatially. (2006). Feuerstein, R. (1980). Gunzelmann, G. (2008). Gyselinck, V., Meneghetti, C., De Beni, R., and Pazzaglia, F. (2009).	Needed for organization and math (rotate this object). Spatial orientation is how objects are represented in space, e.g., a map represents objects in space.
27	144	Teaching adverbs and prepositions	Payne, R. K. (2005).	Very few adverbs or prepositions are used in casual register. Prepositions and adverbs are needed for math, physical education, and social studies, e.g., *up, down, over, under, left, right.*
28	145	Eyes in the visual position	Andreas, F. (1994). Buckner, M., Meara, N. M., Reese, E. J., and Reese, M. (1987).	Neurologically, when eyes are up, the brain is accessing visual information. Important for math.

STRATEGY NUMBER	PAGE NUMBER	ACADEMIC STRATEGIES	RESEARCHERS	EXPLANATION
29	146	Mental model for formal register	Bruce, C., Snodgrass, D., and Salzman, J. A. (1999). Greene, V., and Enfield, M. (1967). Schacter, J. (2001). *Success Stories/ Evidence Data.* (2006). Swan, W. (2007). Wolff, J. (2002). www.ahaprocess.com/ files/R&D_School/ PSM ResearchSummary _2004-2006.pdf	Writing fluency is based upon formal register. This mental model from Project Read enhances fluency and sentence composition. Swan's research data on our work indicate that if the mental model is used consistently, it results in extraordinary writing scores.
30	148	Plan and label	"Annotated Bibliography of MLE, LPAD, & IE, 1990–2005 (including Selected Bibliography of Prof. R. Feuerstein)." (2006). "Mediated Learning Experience in Teaching and Counseling— Proceedings of the International Conferences 'Models of Teaching Training' and 'Educational Advancement for Youth at Risk.'" (2001). Ben-Hur, M. (Ed.). (1994). Feuerstein, R. (1998). Feuerstein, R., et al. (2003). *continued on next page*	Payne's work combines content comprehension and Feuerstein's work on processes. The student can use the vocabulary of the task and can proceduralize the process to get the task done.

STRATEGY NUMBER	PAGE NUMBER	ACADEMIC STRATEGIES	RESEARCHERS	EXPLANATION
30 (continued)	148	Plan and label	Feuerstein, R., Klein, P., and Tannenbaum, A. (Eds.). (1991).	
			Feuerstein, R., Mintzker, Y., Ben-Shachar, N., and Cohen, M. (2001).	
			Feuerstein, R., Rand, Y., and Feuerstein, R. S. (2006).	
			Feuerstein, R., Rand, Y., Falik, L., and Feuerstein, R. S. (2003).	
			Feuerstein, R., Rand, Y., Falik, L., and Feuerstein, R. S. (2006).	
			Feuerstein, S. (2002).	
			Howie, D. R. (2003).	
			Kozulin, A. (2001).	
			Kozulin, A. (Ed.). (1997).	
			Kozulin, A., and Rand, Y. (Eds.). (2000).	
			Lebeer, J. (Ed.). (2003).	
			Mohan, B., and Slater, T. (2006).	
			Payne, R. K. (2005).	
			Seok-Hoon Seng, A., Kwee-Hoon Pou, L., Oon-Seng Tan (Eds.). (2003).	
			Watson, S., and Miller, T. (2009).	
			Woodward-Kron, R. (2008).	

STRATEGY NUMBER	PAGE NUMBER	BEHAVIORAL STRATEGIES	RESEARCHERS	EXPLANATION
31	151	Automaticity	Bloom, B. (1976).	The more complex a process, the more parts of that process have to be automatic. Math facts are an example. In reading, you have to decode at a rate that does not interfere with learning. Sports coaches know that automaticity—the ability to respond automatically—is critical to success. Automaticity requires practice.
32	152	Self-assessment of resources	Devol, P. E. (2004).

DeWitz, S. J., Woolsey, M. L., and Walsh, W. B. (2009).

Krebs, C. (2006).

Vickerstaff, S., Heriot, S., Wong, M., Lopes, A., and Dossetor, D. (2007). | Response to any environment is the ability to name it. When one knows one's own resource base, resources can be leveraged because they can be named. |

STRATEGY NUMBER	PAGE NUMBER	BEHAVIORAL STRATEGIES	RESEARCHERS	EXPLANATION
33	154	Planning for behavior	Agran, M., Blanchard, C., Wehmeyer, M., and Hughes, C. (2001). Coyle, C., and Cole, P. (2004). Feeney, T. J., and Ylvisaker, M. (2008). Feuerstein, R. (1980). Greene, J. A., Moos, D. C., Azevedo, R., and Winters, F. I. (2008). Hamilton, J. L. (2007). King-Sears, M. E. (2008). Kishiyama, M. M., Boyce, W. T., Jimenez, A. M., Perry, L. M., and Knight, R. T. (2008). Mithaug, D. K. (2002). Moore, D. W., Prebble, S., Robertson, J., Waetford, R., and Anderson, A. (2001). Peterson, L. D., Young, K. R., Salzberg, C. L., West, R. P., and Hill, M. (2006).	Planning is related to controlling impulsivity. Also, individuals tend to honor their own plans and not the plans that others make for them.

STRATEGY NUMBER	PAGE NUMBER	BEHAVIORAL STRATEGIES	RESEARCHERS	EXPLANATION
34	156	Building a reward system based on implementing your own plan	Butera, L. M., Giacone, M. V., and Wagner, K. A. (2008). Caine, R. N., and Caine, G. (1991).	Extrinsic rewards work if they are used to start a behavior. Once the behavior is established, extrinsic rewards interfere with the behavior and lessen the behavior. If you tie rewards to the student's ability to complete his/her own plan, then you have established behaviors you want. Once those behaviors are established, then a new plan is made for additional behaviors.
35	157	Affirmations	Dweck, C. (2006). Marzano, R., and Arrendondo, D. (1986). Steiner, C. (1994).	Nurturing, positive self-talk allows for task completion, learning new tasks, etc. Very important in learning.
36	158	Service learning	Billig, S. H. (2002). Brooks, R. (1991). Haskitz, A. (1996).	Giving back to the community in service has very high payoffs in developing resilience and adult capacity.

STRATEGY NUMBER	PAGE NUMBER	BEHAVIORAL STRATEGIES	RESEARCHERS	EXPLANATION
37	159	Peer mediation	Farrell, A. D., Erwin, E. H., Allison, K. W., Meyer, A., Sullivan, T., Camou, S., et al. (2007). Fisher, R., and Ury, W. (1983). Fisher, R., and Ury, W. (1997). Huan, V. S. (2006). Kunsch, C. A., Jitendra, A. K., and Sood, S. (2007). Schellenberg, R. C., Parks-Savage, A., and Rehfuss, M. (2007). Shamir, A., and Lazerovitz, T. (2007). Shamir, A., Tzuriel, D., and Rozen, M. (2006) Traore, R. (2008). Tzuriel, D., and Shamir, A. (2007).	Teaches questioning and the adult voice. Is critical for conflict resolution.
38	160	Storybook to improve behavior	Andreas, S., and Faulkner, C. (1994). Hsu, J. (2008). Seebaum, M. (1999).	Technique developed through drawings and pictures to identify the correct behaviors—especially effective with young children or children with developmental delays.

STRATEGY NUMBER	PAGE NUMBER	BEHAVIORAL STRATEGIES	RESEARCHERS	EXPLANATION
39	161	Metaphor story	Andreas, S., and Faulkner, C. (1994). Freedman, J., and Combs, G. (1996). Hsu, J. (2008).	Technique from neurolinguistic programming (NLP) that uses metaphor story to identify causation behind a particular behavior. See Payne (2005) for more information.
40	163	Adult voice	Berne, E. (1996). Steiner, C. (1994).	Berne identified three voices that one uses inside the head to direct behavior: child voice, adult voice, and parent voice. Steiner found that if an individual became his/her own parent quite young, or if the primary caregiver was unsympathetic, the individual typically only develops two voices—the child and the negative parent. Without an adult voice, it is very difficult to resolve conflicts or maintain healthy relationships.

STRATEGY NUMBER	PAGE NUMBER	BEHAVIORAL STRATEGIES	RESEARCHERS	EXPLANATION
41	166	Classroom management	Evertson, C. M., and Weinstein, C. S. (2006). Schamberg, M. (2008). Simonsen, B., Fairbanks, S., Briesch, A., Myers, D., and Sugai, G. (2008). Stichter, J. P., Lewis, T. J., Whittaker, T. A., Richter, M., Johnson, N. W., and Trussell, R. P. (2009). Walberg, H. J. (1990). Wong, H. K., and Wong, R. T. (1998).	According to Walberg, up to 65% of achievement can be attributed to classroom management. Ninety-five percent of discipline referrals come the first or last five minutes of class because of lack of procedures.

STRATEGY NUMBER	PAGE NUMBER	BOTH BEHAVIORAL AND ACADEMIC STRATEGIES	RESEARCHERS	EXPLANATION
42	171	Art and music instruction	ART: "The Arts and Educational Reform: Ideas for Schools and Communities." (1994). April, A. (2001). Asbury, C., and Rich, B. (Eds.). (2008). Heath, S. B. (2001). Richards, A. G. (2003). MUSIC: Cox, H. A., and Stephens, L. J. (2006). Gouzouasis, P., Guhn, M., and Kishor, N. (2007). Harris, M. (2008). Kinney, D. W. (2008). Piro, J. M., and Ortiz, C. (2009). Rauscher, F. H. (1999). Southgate, D. E., and Roscigno, V. J. (2009).	Both art and music teach students to translate between an abstract symbol (a note, a drawing) and the sensory sound or object it represents. Music also teaches math.

STRATEGY NUMBER	PAGE NUMBER	BOTH BEHAVIORAL AND ACADEMIC STRATEGIES	RESEARCHERS	EXPLANATION
43	173	Reframing	Andreas, S., and Faulkner, C. (1994). Chagnon, F. (2007). Elliott, M., Gray, B., and Lewicki, R. (2003). Elliott, M., Kaufman, S., Gardner, R., and Burgess, G. (2002). Fox, J. E. (1999). Jaser, S. S., Fear, J. M., Reeslund, K. L., Champion, J. E., Reising, M. M., and Compas, B. E. (2008). Mills, A. (1999). Nelson, M. (2000). Peters, G. (2002). Rapee, R. M., Gaston, J. E., and Abbott, M. J. (2009). Reddy, L. A., De Thomas, C. A., Newman, E., and Chun, V. (2009). Riley, L. P., LaMontagne, L. L., Hepworth, J. T., and Murphy, B. A. (2007). Scherff, L., and Singer, N. R. (2008).	This NLP technique is one in which the desired behavior is framed against the individual's identity.

STRATEGY NUMBER	PAGE NUMBER	BOTH BEHAVIORAL AND ACADEMIC STRATEGIES	RESEARCHERS	EXPLANATION
44	174	Relationships of mutual respect	Comer, J. (1995). Ferguson, R. (2008). Goleman, D. (2006). Greenspan, S. I., and Benderly, B. L. (1997). Payne, R. K. (2005).	No significant learning occurs without a significant relationship. In a research study of 910 first-graders, the at-risk students would not learn from the teacher, even with excellent instructional practices, if they perceived the teacher to be cold and controlling. A significant relationship is one of mutual respect that includes high expectations, insistence, and support.

STRATEGY NUMBER	PAGE NUMBER	BOTH BEHAVIORAL AND ACADEMIC STRATEGIES	RESEARCHERS	EXPLANATION
45	175	Planning to control impulsivity	Feuerstein, R. (1980). Schraw, G., Brooks, D., and Crippen, K. J. (2005). Shonkoff, J. P., and Phillips, D. A. (Eds.). (2000).	Feuerstein found that if you cannot plan, you cannot predict. If you cannot predict, you do not know cause and effect. If you do not know cause and effect, you do not know consequence. If you do not know consequence, you do not control impulsivity. If you do not control impulsivity, you have an inclination toward criminal behavior. A neurological study conducted at the University of California, Berkeley, found that poor children's brains have not developed executive functions—one of which is the ability to plan. It can be learned.

STRATEGY NUMBER	PAGE NUMBER	BOTH BEHAVIORAL AND ACADEMIC STRATEGIES	RESEARCHERS	EXPLANATION
46	177	Relational learning * * This strategy has been repeated because of its significance to working with under-resourced learners. It has applications in this area, as well as where it was first introduced.	Domagala-Zysk, E. (2006). Faircloth, B. S., and Hamm, J. V. (2005). Good, M., and Adams, G. R. (2008). Green, G., Rhodes, J., Hirsch, A. H., Suarez-Orozco, C., and Camic, P. M. (2008). Guay, F., Marsh, H. W., Senecal, C., and Dowson, M. (2008). Johnson, Lisa S. (2008). Payne, R. K. (2008). Putnam, R. (2000). Reis, S. M., Colbert, R. D., and Hebert, T. P. (2005). Rimm-Kaufman, S. E., and Chiu, Y.-J. I. (2007). Ross, D. D., Bondy, E., Gallingane, C., and Hambacher, E. (2008). Sanchez, B., Reyes, O., and Singh, J. (2006). Scales, P. C., Benson, P. L., Roehlkepartain, E. C., Sesma, A., Jr., and van Dulmen, M. (2006).	Relational learning involves seven characteristics. See Payne (2008).

STRATEGY NUMBER	PAGE NUMBER	BOTH BEHAVIORAL AND ACADEMIC STRATEGIES	RESEARCHERS	EXPLANATION
47	179	Future story	Adelabu, D. H. (2008). Amyx, D., and Bristow, D. (2004). Bowles, T. (2008). Giota, J. (2006). Greene, B. A., and DeBacker, T. K. (2004). Greene, B. A., Miller, R. B., Crowson, H. M., Duke, B. L., and Akey, K. L. (2004). Horstmanshof, L., and Zimitat, C. (2007). Kaylor, M., and Flores, M. M. (2007). Kerpelman, J. L., Eryigit, S., and Stephens, C. J. (2008). Leondari, A. (2007). Malka, A., and Covington, M. V. (2005). Malmberg, L.-E., Ehrman, J., and Lithen, T. (2005). Phalet, K., Andriessen, I., and Lens, W. (2004). Robbins, R. N., and Bryan, A. (2004). Ryken, A. E. (2006). Seginer, R. (2008). Tabachnick, S. E., Miller, R. B., and Relyea, G. E. (2008).	A future story involves role identity and a future plan that includes education.

STRATEGY NUMBER	PAGE NUMBER	BOTH BEHAVIORAL AND ACADEMIC STRATEGIES	RESEARCHERS	EXPLANATION
48	181	Physical activity	Bailey, R., Armour, K., Kirk, D., Jess, M., Pickup, I., and Sandford, R. (2009). Burton, L. J., VanHeest, J. L. (2007). Chomitz, V. R., Slining, M. M., McGowan, R. J., Mitchell, S. E., Dawson, G. F., and Hacker, K. A. (2009). Ericsson, I. (2008). Ratey, J., and Hageman, E. (2008). Sibley, B. A., Ward, R. M., Yazvac, T. S., Zullig, K., and Potteiger, J. A. (2008). Tomporowski, P. D., Davis, C. L., Miller, P. H., and Naglieri, J. A. (2008). Tremarche, P. V., Robinson, E. M., and Graham, L. B. (2007).	Harvard Research indicates that 45 minutes of exercise at the beginning of the school day significantly raises reading and math scores. The exercise activates brain activity.

STRATEGY NUMBER	PAGE NUMBER	BOTH BEHAVIORAL AND ACADEMIC STRATEGIES	RESEARCHERS	EXPLANATION
49	182	Development of role identity	Barnett, R. C., Gareis, K. C., James, J. B., and Steele, J. (2001). Berzonsky, M. D., Branje, S. J. T., and Meeus, W. (2007). Bianchi, A. J., and Lancianese, D. A. (2005). Britsch, B., and Wakefield, W. D. (1998). Burke, P.J., Owens, T.J., Serpe, R., and Thoits, P. A. (Eds.). (2003). Cinamon, R. G., and Rich, Y. (2002). Desrochers, S. (2002). Diemer, M. A. (2002). Gianakos, I. (1995). Kashima, Y., Foddy, M., and Platow, M. (Eds.). (2002). Pasley, K., Furtis, T. G., and Skinner, M. L. (2002). Razumnikova, O. M. (2005).	Role identity is what you want to do or be; it is one of the most effective tools to prevent early pregnancy.

STRATEGY NUMBER	PAGE NUMBER	BOTH BEHAVIORAL AND ACADEMIC STRATEGIES	RESEARCHERS	EXPLANATION
50	183	Development of appropriate boundaries	Bagby, J. H., Rudd, L. C., and Woods, M. (2005). Burts, D. C., Schmidt, H. M., Durham, R. S., Charlesworth, R., and Hart, C. H. (2007). Covey, S. (1989). Fraser, M. W., Galinsky, M. J., Smokowski, P. R., Day, S. H., Terzian, M. A., Rose, R. A., et al. (2005). Louv, R. (2006). Petermann, F., and Natzke, H. (2008). Vestal, A., and Jones, N. A. (2004).	Appropriate boundaries are a factor in emotional health. These include boundaries in behavior, relationships, verbal comments, judgments, accusations, physical space, physical touch, bullying, and questions. Must be directly taught.
51	184	Response to Intervention (RTI)	"Assisting Students Struggling with Reading: Response to Intervention (RTI) and Multi-Tier Intervention in the Primary Grades." (2009). Haager, D., Klingner, J., and Vaughn, S. (Eds.). (2007). McIntosh, K., Campbell, A. L., Carter, D. R., and Dickey, C. R. (2009). Stewart, R. M., Benner, G. J., Martella, R. C., and Marchand-Martella, N. E. (2007).	Response to Intervention is the federally mandated approach for regular education to address special education student needs. This RTI process is embedded as a form of intervention in the six-step process.

STRATEGY NUMBER	PAGE NUMBER	BOTH BEHAVIORAL AND ACADEMIC STRATEGIES	RESEARCHERS	EXPLANATION
52	185	Six-step process	Payne, R. K. (2008).	The six-step process is a simplified procedure developed by Payne that helps buildings address NCLB (No Child Left Behind) and AYP (adequate yearly progress). The steps are outlined in the book *Under-Resourced Learners.* Payne simplified Lezotte's process, creating a relatively easy way to calculate AYP.
53	186	*The R Rules*	Souther, E. (2008b).	A semester of scripted lessons to use with at-risk secondary students to teach the knowledge bases, self-assess resource bases, learn the hidden rules, etc. Makes a huge difference in achievement. Can be used as a part of homeroom/advisory time.

STRATEGY NUMBER	PAGE NUMBER	COMMUNITY STRATEGIES	RESEARCHERS	EXPLANATION
54	187	Circles™ Campaign	Miller, S. (2007).	A process of building social bridging capital and support systems for adults in poverty.
55	188	*Getting Ahead in a Just-Gettin'-By World*	Devol, P. E. (2004). Devol, P. E. (2006).	A workbook/ program used to develop adult and parent capacity by increasing individual knowledge bases. Individuals in poverty are problem solvers but often don't have the knowledge bases that others have. In a series of 15 lessons people from poverty build knowledge bases. Parents make a future story for themselves and assess their own resource bases.
56	189	Communities in Schools	Barter, B. (2007). Communities in Schools. (2009). Fain, T., Turner, S., and Ridgeway, G. (2008). Hammond, C., Linton, D., Smink, J., and Drew, S. (2007). Milliken, B. (2007).	Started in 1977, Communities in Schools is an after-school program and support system for students. It can be very effective.

STRATEGY NUMBER	PAGE NUMBER	BEHAVIORAL STRATEGIES	RESEARCHERS	EXPLANATION
57	190	*Collaboration For Kids*	Conway, H. W. (2006).	A process developed in Virginia to access all community agencies, judges, law enforcement, etc., to address at-risk behaviors early, with nearly a 90% success rate.

ACADEMIC STRATEGIES

ACADEMIC STRATEGIES	RESEARCHERS	EXPLANATION
Extra time—using technology, scheduling (double periods), or tutors	Bloom, B. (1976). TIME/SCHEDULING: Farbman, D., and Kaplan, C. (2005). Farmer-Hinton, R. L. (2002). Gladwell, M. (2008). Mattox, K., Hancock, D., and Queen, J. A. (2005). TECHNOLOGY: Behrmann, M., and Jerome, M. K. (2002). Swan, K., van Hooft, M., Kratcoski, A., and Unger, D. (2005). Williams, A., Rouse, K., Seals, C., and Gilbert, J. (2009). Wright, J.C., and Huston, A. C. (1995). OTHER: "Report of the National Education Commission on Time and Learning." (1994). Rocha, E. (2008).	Extra time is one of four variables that impact student learning. Using flip video cameras, lessons can be recorded and burned to DVD or stored on a portable device like a laptop or iPod video to be visited again by students. Double periods back to back to increase learning time. Tutors may also be used to provide extra learning time.

EXTRA TIME—USING TECHNOLOGY, SCHEDULING (DOUBLE PERIODS), OR TUTORS

Benjamin Bloom found in his research that the amount of time an individual has to learn something makes a big difference in achievement. Malcolm Gladwell (2008) calls it the 10,000-hour guideline, i.e., to be an expert in something requires 10,000 hours working in that occupation or knowledge base. Numerous studies link time on task in a classroom to the achievement in that classroom. Extra time can be provided by using technology (downloadable audio and video files of the teacher teaching), double scheduling time, tutors, etc.

STRATEGY

ACADEMIC STRATEGIES	RESEARCHERS	EXPLANATION
Content comprehension (structure, purpose, pattern, process of the discipline)	Bransford, J. D., Brown, A. L., and Cocking, R. R. (Eds.). (2000). Donovan, M. S., and Bransford, J. D. (2005). Hill, H. C., Blunk, M. L., Charalambous, Y., Lewis, J. M., Phelps, G. C., Sleep, L., and Ball, D. L. (2008). Kilpatrick, J., Swafford, J., and Findell, B. (Eds.). (2001). Krauss, S., Brunner, M., Kunter, M., Baumert, J., Neubrand, M., Blum, W., et al. (2008). Senge, P. (1994). Shulman, L. (1987).	All content has a purpose, as well as structures, patterns, and processes. That is the basis for determining what is and is not important in the discipline. These can be represented by concept maps, mental models, and visual representations.

WHAT IS CONTENT COMPREHENSION?

Just as reading comprehension means that you understand the reading passage, so content comprehension means you understand the content at a level where you can manipulate it and use it.

To use and manipulate content, in addition to knowing the meaning of vocabulary, you also must know the purpose, structures, patterns, and processes used in that particular discipline or content. These four factors tell you what is more important and less important as you sort information in order to use it.

For example, the purpose of language arts is to study how structure and language are used to influence a reader. It is basically about writers and readers. The structures are the genres (short story, drama, poetry, biography, novels, etc.), grammar, organizational patterns of text, syllables, phonics, etc. The patterns then become units of study.

54

The processes can include reading, writing, speaking, filmmaking, and listening. So an expert teacher in language arts is going to help his/her students understand that language arts is always about the relationship between reader and writer—the manipulations of structure, word choice, organization, etc.—in that process.

Another example: Math is about assigning order and value to the universe. We use numbers, space, and time as primary structures to do that. Patterns that are taught include fractions (part to whole of space), decimals (part to whole of numbers), measurement (assigning the value of space and time). Processes are addition, subtraction, multiplication, and division. So an elementary school teacher would facilitate a discussion with students about how to know how much space is theirs in a classroom before introducing fractions. The class would measure the room, divide it with masking tape, and calculate space using fractions. The teacher could do the same thing by dividing pizza. The students would then understand what each student needs to know about measurement and fractions.

For example, the purpose of chemistry is to understand chemical bonding. The periodic table provides the rules or patterns for bonding. The process used to figure out the bonding is equations. The structure theory has varied from shell theory to vapor cloud theory to string theory.

When students have content comprehension, teachers can spend the majority of their time teaching the use and manipulation of the content. For example, in language arts in high school, the teacher does not test by asking what color the girl's dress was in the story, but rather "What specific techniques did the writer use to make the reader feel empathetic toward the girl?" Or: "How would the reader have felt different if this short story had been told in a poem?"

Lee Shulman found that this was a critical issue in excellent teaching. Furthermore, he indicated that graphic visual representations (mental models) used by the teacher came out of this understanding—and that teachers then knew when a student had a slight misunderstanding versus no understanding at all.

And it also can be stated that if teachers don't understand their content against these four criteria—purpose, structures, patterns, and processes—they can't facilitate or develop high achievement. It's impossible to teach what you don't know.

STRATEGY

ACADEMIC STRATEGIES	RESEARCHERS	EXPLANATION
Mental models for academic content	Baghban, M. (2007). Bailey, M., et.al. (1995). Donovan, M. S., and Bransford, J. D. (2005). Guastello, E. F., Beasley, T. M., and Sinatra, R. C., (2000). Herman, T., Colton, S., and Franzen, M. (2008). Idol, L., and Jones, B.F. (1991). Jones, B. F., Pierce, J., Hunter, B. (1988). Kilpatrick, J., Swafford, J., and Findell, B. (Eds.). (2001). Lin, H., and Chen, T. (2006). Marzano, R. (2007). Marzano, R., and Arrendondo, D. (1986). McCrudden, M. T., Schraw, G., and Lehman, S. (2009). Payne, R. K. (2005). Payne, R. K. (2007). Resnick, L., and Klopfer, L. (1989). Schnotz, W., and Kurschner, C. (2008). Senge, P. (1994). Shulman, L. (1987).	Mental models are drawings, stories, and analogies that translate ideas into sensory representations or experiences that help make sense of information and increase memory of information.

MENTAL MODELS

To translate the concrete to the abstract, the mind needs to hold the information in a mental model. A mental model can be a two-dimensional visual representation, a story, a metaphor, or an analogy.

To understand any discipline or field of study, one must understand the mental models that the discipline uses. In effect, virtually all disciplines are based on mental models. For example, when an individual builds a house, many discussions and words (the abstract) are used to convey what the finished house (the concrete) will be. But between the words and the finished house are blueprints. Blueprints are the translators. Between the three-dimensional concrete house and the abstract words, a two-dimensional visual translates.

When mental models are directly taught, abstract information can be learned much more quickly and retained because the mind has a way to contain it or hold it.

One of the most important mental models for students to have is a mental model for time that includes past, present, and future. A mental model for time is vital to understanding cause, effect, consequence, and sequence. Without a model for time, an individual cannot plan. (Please note that there are cultural differences in mental models for time; however, all cultural mental models for time do have a way to address past, present, and future.)

To access a student's mental model in a particular instance, use sketching or ask for a story, analogy, or metaphor. Sketching is a particularly useful tool in better understanding what a student has stored in terms of mental models. To do sketching with students, have them draw a two-dimensional visual of how they think about a word, an idea, a person, etc.

WHAT ARE MENTAL MODELS?

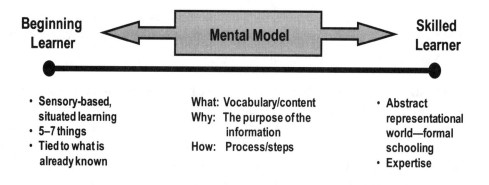

| Beginning Learner | Mental Model | Skilled Learner |

- Sensory-based, situated learning
- 5–7 things
- Tied to what is already known

What: Vocabulary/content
Why: The purpose of the information
How: Process/steps

- Abstract representational world—formal schooling
- Expertise

When a great discrepancy exists between the way the learner creates understanding and the way the expert communicates understanding, failure results.

EXPLANATION

This diagram shows that to translate the concrete to the abstract the mind needs to hold the information in a mental model. A mental model can be a two-dimensional visual representation, a story, a metaphor, or an analogy.

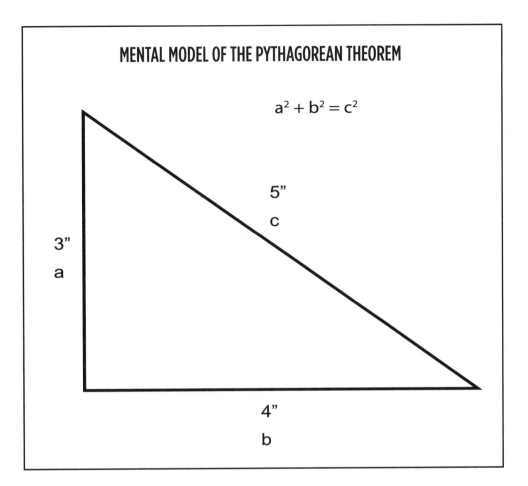

EXPLANATION

$a^2 + b^2 = c^2$

Pythagorean Theorem is a theory of relationship and proportion. In other words, if you know two sides of a right angle triangle, you can know the third side.

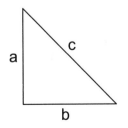

The Pythagorean Theorem is $a^2 + b^2 = c^2$. This diagram represents the geometric proof of the formula.

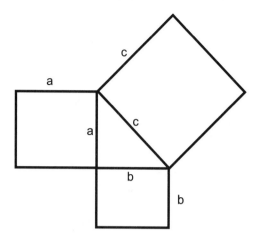

What the theorem is stating is that if you square the length of side a (represented by the square with side lengths of a) and square the length of side b (represented by the square with side lengths of b), the combined area of the two squares will equal the area of square of side c (represented by the square with side lengths of c).

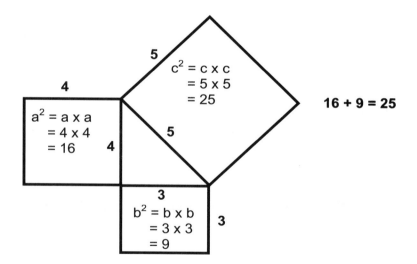

Therefore, the length of each side of the right triangle is the square root of the area of that side squared.

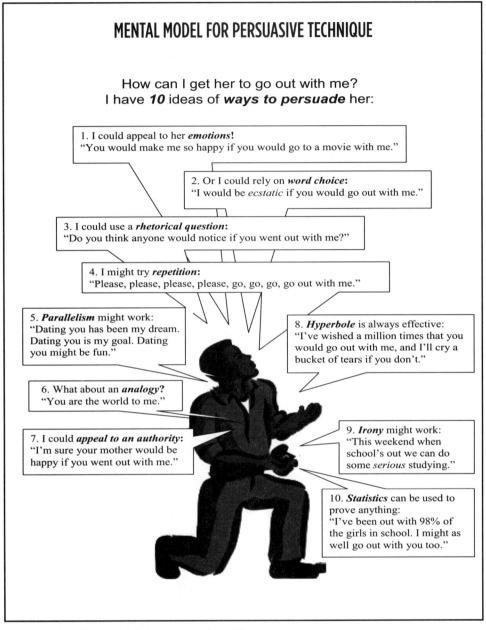

MENTAL MODEL FOR PERSUASIVE TECHNIQUE

How can I get her to go out with me?
I have **10** ideas of **ways to persuade** her:

1. I could appeal to her **emotions**!
"You would make me so happy if you would go to a movie with me."

2. Or I could rely on **word choice**:
"I would be *ecstatic* if you would go out with me."

3. I could use a **rhetorical question**:
"Do you think anyone would notice if you went out with me?"

4. I might try **repetition**:
"Please, please, please, please, go, go, go, go out with me."

5. **Parallelism** might work:
"Dating you has been my dream. Dating you is my goal. Dating you might be fun."

6. What about an **analogy**?
"You are the world to me."

7. I could **appeal to an authority**:
"I'm sure your mother would be happy if you went out with me."

8. **Hyperbole** is always effective:
"I've wished a million times that you would go out with me, and I'll cry a bucket of tears if you don't."

9. **Irony** might work:
"This weekend when school's out we can do some *serious* studying."

10. **Statistics** can be used to prove anything:
"I've been out with 98% of the girls in school. I might as well go out with you too."

Source: *Mental Models for English/Language Arts: Grades 6–12*

61

MENTAL MODEL FOR PLACE VALUE

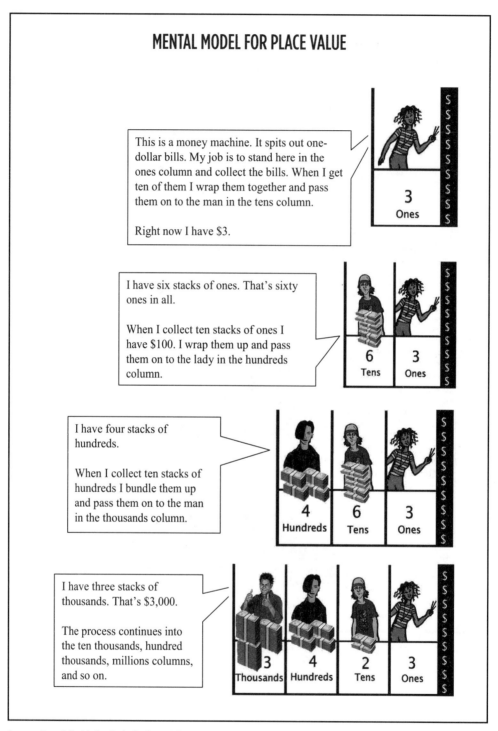

This is a money machine. It spits out one-dollar bills. My job is to stand here in the ones column and collect the bills. When I get ten of them I wrap them together and pass them on to the man in the tens column.

Right now I have $3.

I have six stacks of ones. That's sixty ones in all.

When I collect ten stacks of ones I have $100. I wrap them up and pass them on to the lady in the hundreds column.

I have four stacks of hundreds.

When I collect ten stacks of hundreds I bundle them up and pass them on to the man in the thousands column.

I have three stacks of thousands. That's $3,000.

The process continues into the ten thousands, hundred thousands, millions columns, and so on.

Source: *Mental Models for Math: Grades 6–12*

MENTAL MODEL FOR POSITIVE AND NEGATIVE NUMBERS

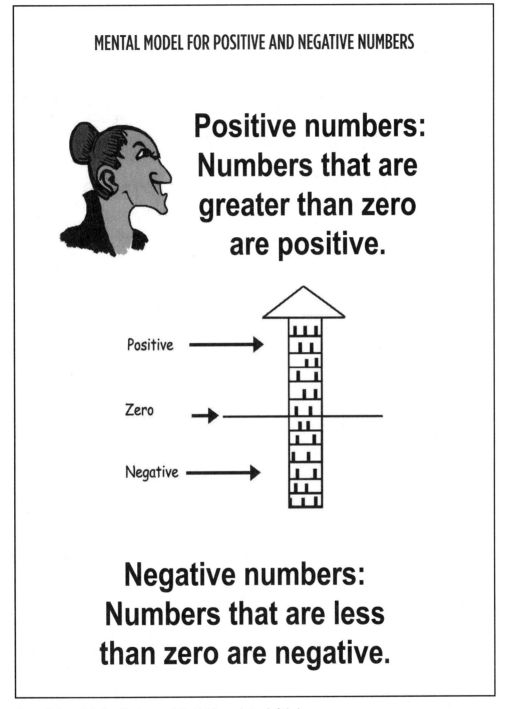

Positive numbers: Numbers that are greater than zero are positive.

Positive →

Zero →

Negative →

Negative numbers: Numbers that are less than zero are negative.

Source: Bethanie H. Tucker, *The Journey of Al and Gebra to the Land of Algebra*

STRATEGY

ACADEMIC STRATEGIES	RESEARCHERS	EXPLANATION
Composing questions	Campbell, T. (2006). Chin, C., and Kayalvizhi, G. (2002). Chin, C., and Osborne, J. (2008). del Mar Badia Martin, M., Gotzens Busquet, C., Genovard Rossello, C., and Castelló Tarrida, A. (2007). Dermody, M. M., Speaker, R. B., Jr. (1999). McManus, D. O., Dunn, R., and Denig, S. J. (2003). National Institute of Child Health and Human Development. (2000). Palincsar, A., and Brown, A. L. (1984). Parker, M., and Hurry, J. (2007). Walberg, H. (1990). Whalon, K., and Hanline, M. F. (2008).	If students say, "I don't understand," and you ask what part don't they understand, and they say, "All of it," or "None of it," they probably cannot ask a question syntactically. Palincsar correlated it with reading achievement. Walberg gave it an effect size of .35—i.e., test scores are one third higher on average.

QUESTION MAKING

To be able to formulate questions syntactically is very important because without this ability the mind literally cannot know what it knows. Many students will ask questions through their tone of voice (e.g., "You don't *have* any more??"). That is a statement that the voice tone has made into a question. If they cannot examine their own behavior, then the students syntactically or grammatically make it into a question (e.g., "Don't you have any more?"). Or they ask it in the formal register of their native language.

To do any task, one must be able to go inside the head and ask questions. If individuals cannot, then they cannot examine any behavior, nor can they retrieve information in a systematic way. For example, if a teacher says to a student, "Why did you do that?" and the student replies, "I don't know," then the teacher needs to see if the student can ask questions syntactically or in formal register. Chances are very good that the student is saying to himself inside his head, "I did that?"

One of the most important cognitive skills to teach students is having them ask the questions. There are several ways to do this, including:

1. Play "Jeopardy!" This exercise involves you giving the answer, and the student needs to come up with the question.
2. For young students, have them start the first word of a sentence with one of the following words: who, what, when, where, which, how.
3. Have students write their own questions with multiple-choice answers.
4. Use question stems for reading, math, and science.
5. Using a multiple-choice test, have students tell you why the incorrect answers are wrong. (While this doesn't give students the ability to ask questions syntactically, it does teach them how to identify wrong answers.)

WRITING MULTIPLE-CHOICE QUESTIONS

Question:

a.
b.
c.
d.

Three Rules:

1. One wrong-answer choice must be funny.
2. Only one answer choice can be right.
3. May not use "all of the above," "none of the above," etc.

EXPLANATION

If twice a week, instead of having students answer the questions at the end of the chapter you have them write the questions, their test scores will "shoot up." Use this form to have students develop their own multiple choice questions. They must follow the three rules listed at the bottom of the form.

Begin by having students write their questions, then debrief with them about how their questions are written.

Question making is developmental. But if by the end of second grade students still cannot ask questions, it will probably impact their reading.

If you have a child who cannot ask a question syntactically, then the student likely will not get past the third grade reading level.
Hint: Sometimes in poverty when a child asks questions, he/she might get slapped.

In second grade have only two answer choices: one right and one wrong.

If you teach a child how to write questions and answer them, you can expect to raise test scores by a third.

If twice a week, instead of having students answer the questions at the end of the chapter, you have them write the questions, their test scores should shoot up.

Not only will their scores go up, you also have developed cognitive capacity (the ability to ask questions).

Anne Marie Palincsar, who did reciprocal teaching, said that if students can ask questions syntactically, their reading is much better.

Debriefing original questions:
- What is the question asking?
- Is there a right answer?
- Is there more than one right answer?
- Do we need a qualifier?

MATH QUESTIONS

1. Stems (see explanation below) need to use the terminology.
2. Distracters are:
   - Incorrect operation
   - Incorrect order
   - Decimal in wrong place
   - Answer in wrong form (percentage instead of number, etc.)
   - Missed step
   - Unnecessary information included
   - Computational errors

EXPLANATION

Test makers call the question part the stem; the answer choices are called the distracters.

In writing math questions, you want to make sure in your question stems that you have the terminology that is being used.

Errors students might make (in trying to come up with an answer) include the following:
- Added all the numbers together
- Used the wrong operation
- Missed information

Have students identify why the wrong answer is wrong.

Have students write questions twice a week. If they do, their test scores rise.

If you have students who cannot ask questions syntactically, they cannot plan. Further, they cannot resolve conflict, and they don't know what they do know and what they don't know.

SCIENCE QUESTION/WRITING STEMS

How for the Student	Question Stem
Defining and describing	**Knowledge** • What is (are) ... • Where is (are) ... • Which is (are) ... • How is (are) ... **Comprehension** • What conclusions can you draw from ... • What observations did you make? **Application** • Why does ... work? • Sketch your mental model of ... **Analysis** • Explain how ... **Synthesis** • How could you explain ... to your friend? • Design a model of ... to represent ... • Write a letter to ... giving a summary of ... • What facts can you compile about ... • Rewrite the definition of ... in your own words. **Evaluation** • Describe the importance of ...
Representing data and interpreting representations	**Knowledge** • Describe what happens when ... **Comprehension** • Describe what happens when ... • Construct a model to explain your data ... **Application** • How could you organize your data to help you draw your conclusion? • How could you change the process/procedure to increase/decrease the ... **Analysis** • How can you sort the parts of ... • What order can you place the data in to make them easier to interpret? **Synthesis** • How could you compile the data/facts for ... • What plan do you have for collecting your data? • What format will you use to represent your data? **Evaluation** • What data will you use to evaluate ... • How could you verify the interpretation of your graph/table/map? • What is your interpretation of your data?

SCIENCE QUESTION/WRITING STEMS (continued)

How for the Student	Question Stem
Identifying and classifying	**Knowledge** • How could you recognize ... **Comprehension** • How could you differentiate between ... and ... **Application** • Determine what characteristics/properties you can use to identify ... **Analysis** • Identify the characteristics of ... and compare them to the characteristics of ... **Synthesis** • Devise a new way to classify ... • What other ways can ... be identified? **Evaluation** • What criteria would you use to assess the ... classification system?
Measuring: ordering/ comparing along a continuum	**Knowledge** • What qualitative data did you record? **Application** • When compared along the continuum of ..., how can ... be ordered? **Synthesis** • Develop a plan/grid to record your observations for ... • How could you arrange your groups differently? **Evaluation** • What qualitative data were used to evaluate ... • What is your interpretation of the data gathered when ...
Measuring: qualifying	**Knowledge** • What qualitative data did you record? **Application** • How can you organize your data? **Synthesis** • What properties remained constant when ... • What properties changed when ... **Evaluation** • Develop a plan/table to record your observations for ... • How could you arrange your data differently?
Predicting/ inferring	**Knowledge** • What do you know about ... **Comprehension** • What clues do you have about .... **Application** • What would be the result of ... **Analysis** • What do you think happened from the data about ... **Synthesis** • Predict the outcome of ... if ... **Evaluation** • What choices would you have made if you could ... • What changes could be made to alter ... • How could you verify what you have inferred?

SCIENCE QUESTION/WRITING STEMS (continued)

How for the Student	Question Stem
Posing questions	**Knowledge** • How is (are) ... • What is (are) ... • Where is (are) ... • Which is ... • When did ... • Who is (are) ... **Comprehension** • List what you know and what you want to learn about ... • Using the CPR (capitalization, punctuation, restatement) model, write a question about ... **Application** • What actions would you have to take to test your question? • Where can you find more information concerning your question? **Analysis** • Explain how your questions ask about causes and effects. • How is ... in your question connected to ...? **Synthesis** • What changes would you make to revise ... **Evaluation** • What criteria could you use to assess if your question is testable?
Designing and conducting investigations	**Knowledge** • Identify the materials you would need to conduct your investigation. **Comprehension** • What is the responding/dependent variable in your investigation? **Application** • How will you organize your data for ... **Analysis** • What did you observe during your investigation? **Synthesis** • What changes could you make to your investigation to ... **Evaluation** • What data were most important to prove or disprove your hypothesis?
Constructing evidence-based explanations	**Knowledge** • What scientific theories/models/principles are related to your explanation? **Comprehension** • How could you explain ... **Synthesis** • What alternative hypotheses are there for ... **Evaluation** • How will you assess all the hypotheses to verify or dispute?

SCIENCE QUESTION/WRITING STEMS (continued)

How for the Student	Question Stem
Analyzing and interpreting data	**Knowledge** • What data would you choose to analyze? **Comprehension** • Translate the data in your table to a graph. **Application** • What do the collected data mean? **Analysis** • How do the data help you answer your question? • What patterns do you find in ... **Synthesis** • What other factors could be measured for ... **Evaluation** • How could you verify your interpretation?
Evaluating/ reflecting/ making an argument	**Knowledge** • What data do you have to support your argument? **Comprehension** • Explain your argument. **Application** • How could you develop ... to represent ... **Analysis** • Do your data support your argument? **Synthesis** • How could this model of ... be revised to represent ... **Evaluation** • Does this model follow or "obey" the theory or argument?

Developed by Terry Ross

Works cited:

Lujan, Michael L. (2006) Critical Thinking–Bloom's Taxonomy Mentoring Minds. Tyler, TX.

Smith, C., Wiser, M., Anderson, C. and Krajcik, J. (2006). (Focus article of combined double issue of journal): Implications of Research on Children's Learning for Standards and Assessment: A Proposed Learning Progression for Matter and Atomic-Molecular Theory. Measurement, 14 (1&2), 1–98.

Texas Administrative Code (TAC), Title 19, Part II Chapter 112. Texas Essential Knowledge and Skills for Science.

QUESTION STEMS FOR
FIFTH- AND NINTH-GRADE READING

1. In paragraph _____, what does _____ mean?
2. Paragraph _____ is mainly about _____.
3. From the article, the reader can tell …
4. From the passage, the reader can tell …
5. From the paragraph, the reader can tell …
6. From what the reader learns about _____, which statement does not make sense?
7. How does _____ feel?
8. Why is it important …
9. Which of these is the best summary of the selection?
10. Look at this web (flow chart, graph, charts, etc.). Which detail belongs in the empty space?
11. An idea present in both selections is …
12. One way these selections are alike is …
13. One way these selections are different is …
14. Paragraph _____ is important because it helps the reader understand …
15. The reader can tell when _____, he/she will probably …
16. How does _____ feel?
17. In paragraph _____, why is _____ sad? (happy, confused, angry, etc.)
18. What is this article mainly about?
19. What can the reader tell about _____ from information in this article?
20. The author builds suspense by …
21. One way this story resembles a fable is that …
22. In paragraph _____, the author uses the word _____ to emphasize _____.
23. Which of the following words is a synonym (antonym) for the word _____ in paragraph _____?
24. What is the overall theme expressed in this article?
25. Which of the following sentences from the article explains the author's primary conflict?
26. The audience that would probably relate most to the article's central message would be …
27. Why …
28. How ...

Adapted from TAKS (Texas Assessment of Knowledge and Skills)

EXPLANATION

Put students in pairs and give one of these pages and stems for them to use to write questions.

Analyze questions from your state assessment and compile stems appropriate to it.

SOCIAL STUDIES QUESTION STEM STARTERS

Elementary (K–4)

1. What does the map (chart, drawing, timeline, graph) illustrate?
2. Which statement BEST explains (summarizes) _____?
3. What was the main cause of _____?
4. One advantage of _____ is _____.
5. The primary function (purpose, goal, objective) of _____ is _____.
6. Which of the following were consequences of _____?
7. What is the BEST definition of _____?
8. Which of these is a past (current) trend in _____?
9. Approximately when did _____ occur?
10. Which date is associated with _____?
11. Which of these statements explains how _____?
12. What is an example of _____?
13. Which of these would be the BEST solution to _____?
14. What was (person's) major accomplishment?
15. Who is BEST known for _____?
16. Which BEST explains what happened in _____?
17. Who was _____?
18. What person (event, element, condition) was responsible for _____?
19. What happened when _____?
20. What can be concluded from the visual aid?
21. Who made a factual statement about the _____?
22. What document includes the ideas represented in the diagram?
23. What happened at the beginning, middle, end of the story/event?
24. What picture or event goes first, second, next, last?
25. What happened first, second, next, last on the timeline?
26. How are you alike or different from the character in the story or historical event?
27. What happened long ago, yesterday, or today on the timeline, in the story/event?
28. How many days, weeks, months, years, decades, centuries did it take to _____?
29. What natural and/or man-made features played a role in _____?
30. What natural and/or man-made features were near, next to, north, south of _____?
31. What features/characteristics can you identify in the picture, on the map?
32. What would you see, taste, hear, touch, smell if you were "in the shoes" of the person/character?
33. What questions would you like to ask the person about _____?
34. How would things have turned out differently if the character in a historical story, legend, myth, or narrative had acted differently?
35. How are the two historical sources alike and how are they different?
36. What was a problem people had in _____ and how is that alike or different from a problem we have today?
37. What characters, events, or dates should be grouped together and why should they be grouped together?
38. What words help you understand where, when the story, event happened?

Remember: Many of the above questions can be reconfigured into negative questions, e.g., #18 What person (event, element, condition) was NOT responsible for _____?

Developed by Connie Abernathy

SOCIAL STUDIES QUESTION STEM STARTERS

Secondary (Grades 5–12)

1. How are different ways of life determined by location?
2. How do/did _____ adapt to their environment?
3. How are/were the roles of the _____ different from the _____?
4. What circumstances led to changes in the lives of _____?
5. What would happen to the _____ civilization if _____?
6. How are the _____ and the _____ similar and different?
7. What connects the grouping?
8. What was the response by _____ to the _____?
9. How did the actions of _____ conflict with _____?
10. How did the _____ feel about _____?
11. What is the correct sequence for the events?
12. What are the connections between the events listed/shown?
13. What contributed the MOST to _____?
14. What are _____ reasons for _____?
15. What are _____ causes of/for _____?
16. What are _____ effects of/for the _____?
17. Why do you think the _____ was successful or unsuccessful?
18. Between which years did the number increase/decrease/remain the same? What explains this answer?
19. What was the status of _____ before/after the _____?
20. How did the presence of _____ affect the _____?
21. What is the relative/absolute location of _____?
22. How was propaganda used during _____?
23. What determines whether an event is labeled as a "turning point"?
24. How did the _____ and the _____ affect the _____?
25. What are "primary resources" and why are they important?
26. How would your life be different today if _____?
27. How are the maps, events, and/or people similar and different?
28. What is the difference between a primary source and secondary source?
29. What were (person's) problems and how successful or unsuccessful were attempts to resolve each problem?
30. Which opinion would you judge valid, unacceptable? Why?
31. What actions taken by _____ led to _____?
32. Do you agree or disagree with _____? Why?
33. What is the writer's point of view?

Developed by Connie Abernathy

STRATEGY

ACADEMIC STRATEGIES	RESEARCHERS	EXPLANATION
Procedural self-talk	Callicott, K. J., and Park, H. (2003). Fernyhough, C., and Fradley, E. (2005). Feuerstein, R. (1980). Kishiyama, M. M., Boyce, W. T., Jimenez, A. M., Perry L. M., and Knight, R. T. (2008). Manfra, L., and Winsler, A. (2006). Ostad, S. A., and Askeland, M. (2008). Stamou, E., Theodorakis, Y., Kokaridas, D., Perkos, S., and Kessanopoulou, M. (2007).	To complete tasks involves prefrontal activity—planning. Planning requires procedural self-talk. Because the executive functions of some poor children's brains are less developed, planning and self-talk can be directly taught using games and procedural tools.

SELF-TALK

A student needs positive self-talk and procedural self-talk to do well at work and school. Procedural self-talk comes from being able to plan. If students cannot plan, they will not have procedural self-talk, i.e., "First I need to do this, then this, then this, etc." Step sheets of the order that must be followed to do something are very important.

STRATEGY

ACADEMIC STRATEGIES	RESEARCHERS	EXPLANATION
Nonfiction reading strategy (input process)	Feuerstein, R. (1980). Gaddy, S. A., Bakken, J. P., and Fulk, B. M. (2008). Gajria, M., Jitendra, A. K., Sood, S., and Sacks, G. (2007). Hall, K. M., Sabey, B. L., and McClellan, M. (2005). McCrudden, M. T., Schraw, G., and Lehman, S. (2009). Montelongo, J., Berber-Jimenez, L., Hernandez, A. C., and Hosking, D. (2006). National Institute of Child Health and Human Development. (2000). Rogevich, M. E., and Perin, D. (2008). van den Bos, K. P., Nakken, H., Nicolay, P. G., and van Houten, E. J. (2007). Williams, J. P., Hall, K. M., Lauer, K. D., Stafford, K. B., DeSisto, L. A., and deCani, J. S. (2005). Williams, J. P., Stafford, K. B., Lauer, K. D., Hall, K. M., and Pollini, S. (2009).	To complete a task requires a systematic approach.

NONFICTION READING

Most state assessments have gone to a high percentage of the text being nonfiction. Inside your head, you sort nonfiction differently from fiction.

READING STRATEGIES

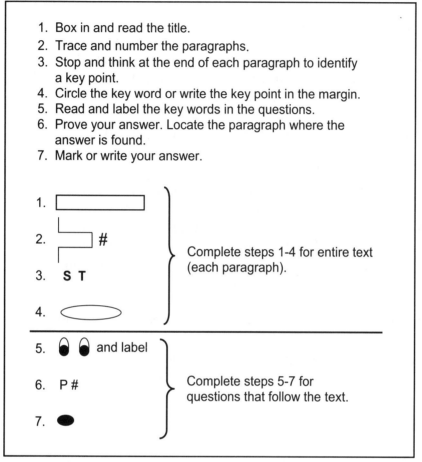

1. Box in and read the title.
2. Trace and number the paragraphs.
3. Stop and think at the end of each paragraph to identify a key point.
4. Circle the key word or write the key point in the margin.
5. Read and label the key words in the questions.
6. Prove your answer. Locate the paragraph where the answer is found.
7. Mark or write your answer.

1.

2. #

Complete steps 1-4 for entire text (each paragraph).

3. **S T**

4.

5. and label

Complete steps 5-7 for questions that follow the text.

6. P #

7.

Source: Kim D. Ellis, *Putting the Pieces Together*

EXPLANATION

Use these reading strategies with the article "The Wonder of Mughal Agra" and with the questions that follow the article.

"Plan and label" means you have a way to go through something systematically, and you have a way to label it or assign words to it so that you can repeat it.

Feuerstein (1980) found in his research that when individuals do not have a systematic way to do anything (or a task), they miss up to 50% of the original data.

Step #1:   Box in the title and the subtitles.

Step #2:   Outline paragraphs by indenting wherever the paragraph indents.

Step #3:   Number the paragraphs.

Step #4:   Go back and circle one word (no more than two words) that indicate what the paragraph is mostly about. Circle the word or words that get referred to most. It is the number of times a word gets referred to that makes it a word you would circle.

Step #5:   Put a pair of eyeballs and a question mark by the key words in each question, which means to read and label the key words in the questions.

Step #6:   Read the questions. Tell students to "X" out at least two answers that they know are not correct.

Step #7:   Bubble in the right answer and put the number of the paragraph that contained the right answer. If the answer choice came out of only one paragraph, it cannot be the summary.

Have students put the number of the paragraph next to the question that it answers.

Have students write a summary for each circled word.

THE WONDER OF MUGHAL AGRA

The Taj Mahal, one of the world's wonders, represents the architectural achievement of India during centuries of Muslim rule. The Mughal emperor Shah Jahan achieved the height of creation with the construction of a mausoleum, or tomb, for his wife, the empress Mumtaz Mahal.

They were married in 1612, and Shah Jahan became emperor in 1628. Devoted to each other, Mumtaz and the emperor traveled everywhere together, including the battlefield. On June 28, 1631, Mumtaz died while giving birth to their 14th child. Every Friday for six months Shah Jahan visited her temporary grave until construction began for her tomb in nearby Agra, a city located along a river.

Shah Jahan gathered the finest talent in his empire for the construction of the tomb. Individual artists and craftsmen worked with white and yellow marble, sandstone, diamonds, and other precious and semi-precious stones from as far away as China. An immense amount of labor was necessary; the workers were housed near the building site. The Taj Mahal took 22 years to build and was completed in 1648. The word "taj" means a high, conical hat worn in Islamic countries.

The Taj Mahal was more than just a tomb. It was also a setting for people to come and pay their respects to Mumtaz Mahal. The design of the site had to accommodate thousands of people and handle ceremonies connected with the anniversaries of the empress's death. A large rectangle was measured along the river and divided into two unequal parts. The mosque and tomb were placed in the larger portion on a raised terrace overlooking the river. The mausoleum was placed on the terrace, according to the emperor's instructions. A large gateway at the southern end was the only public entrance.

Shah Jahan, who created the Taj Mahal in memory of his beloved wife, died February 3, 1666. He was laid to rest in the vault on Mumtaz Mahal's right. He of course had no idea that the tribute to his wife would become a site visited by people from around the world for centuries after his own death.

1. What BEST describes the length of Muslim rule in India?

   A   More than 200 years
   B   Less than 100 years
   C   22 years
   D   From 1612 to 1666

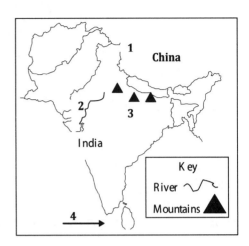

2. Based on the reading, what is the meaning of the word mausoleum?

   F   Architecture
   G   Rectangle
   H   Tomb
   J   Wonder

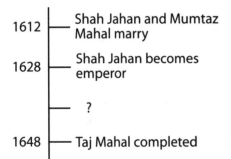

1612	Shah Jahan and Mumtaz Mahal marry
1628	Shah Jahan becomes emperor
	?
1648	Taj Mahal completed

3. What event BEST completes the timeline above?

   A   Shah Jahan dies
   B   Shah Jahan visits the temporary grave site
   C   Agra is built
   D   Muslims ruled India

4. Based on the map above, what is the MOST LIKELY location for the Taj Mahal?

   F   1
   G   2
   H   3
   J   4

5. The term Mughal emperor is BEST connected with:

   A   Rule of China by Mumtaz Mahal
   B   Shah Janhan's rule of the Taj Mahal
   C   The design and purpose of the Taj Mahal
   D   Muslim rule of India

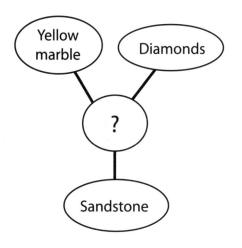

6. What is the correct title for the web shown above?

   F Agra buildings
   G Muslim rule
   H Construction materials
   J Artists and craftsmen

7. In addition to acting as a tomb, what else did the design have to accommodate?

   A Large number of people
   B Chinese architecture
   C Mausoleum law
   D Muslim rule of India

8. The Taj Mahal did NOT act as a:
   F Mausoleum
   G Ceremonial site
   H School
   J Mosque

9. What statement is NOT true about the Taj Mahal?

   A There is only one public entrance
   B Mumtaz Mahal is buried to the right of her husband
   C The mausoleum is on a raised terrace overlooking the river
   D Shah Jahan is buried there

10. What BEST summarizes the article?

   F Mughal emperors controlled China for a very long time
   G Provided details for measurements, construction, and design for a famous site
   H Design and purpose of the Taj Mahal inspired people
   J Shah Jahan and Mumtaz needed space for all their children

81

STRATEGY

ACADEMIC STRATEGIES	RESEARCHERS	EXPLANATION
Problem-solving process (input process)	Boulware-Gooden, R., Carreker, S., Thornhill, A., and Joshi, R. M. (2007). Feuerstein, R. (1980). Fuchs, L. S., Fuchs, D., Prentice, K., Hamlett, C. L., Finelli, R., and Courey, S. J. (2004). Morrison, J. A., and Young, T. A., (2008). Schraw, G., Brooks, D., and Crippen, K. J. (2005). Singh, C. (2008). Star, J. R., and Rittle-Johnson, B. (2008).	To complete a task requires a systematic approach.

PROBLEM-SOLVING PROCESS

Any process requires a systematic approach in order to do it. Without a systematic approach, it is possible, according to Feuerstein (as noted previously), to miss up to 50% of the data. What this process for math problem solving does is provide a systematic approach.

PROBLEM-SOLVING PROCESS

Step 1: **READ THE PROBLEM**
- Read the problem through completely to get a general idea of what the problem is asking.

Step 2: **REREAD THE PROBLEM AND QUESTION**
- Reread to visualize the problem.
- Highlight or mark the question with a wavy line.

Step 3: **MARK YOUR INFORMATION**
- Mark the important information and eliminate unnecessary information.

- Box the action or important words.

- Circle needed information.

- Loop out extra information. *eeeeeee*

Step 4: **CHOOSE AN APPROPRIATE STRATEGY**
- Choose an operation (+ - x ÷).
- Solve a simpler problem.
- Make an organized list.
- Look for a pattern.
- Use logical reasoning.
- Guess and check.
- Make a table.
- Use objects.
- Draw a picture.
- Act it out.
- Work backwards.

Step 5: **SOLVE**
- Solve the problem.

Step 6: **IS THE QUESTION ANSWERED?**
- Read the question again.
- Does the solution answer the question?
- Does it make sense? Is it reasonable?
- Check by using a different strategy if possible.

Source: Judy Sain, *Daily Math Skills Review*

STRATEGY

ACADEMIC STRATEGIES	RESEARCHERS	EXPLANATION
Step sheets (input process)	Beatham, M. D. (2009). Feuerstein, R. (1980). Krueger, K. A., and Dayan, P. (2009). Lodewyk, K. R., Winne, P. H., and Jamieson-Noel, D. L. (2009). Marzano, R., and Arrendondo, D. (1986). Ngu, B. H., Mit, E., Shahbodin, F., and Tuovinen, J. (2009).	To complete tasks requires planning, which requires procedural self-talk. Because the executive functions of some poor children's brains are less developed, planning and self-talk can be directly taught using games and procedural tools.

STEP SHEETS

Step sheets provide procedural information for academic tasks. As noted, if students cannot plan, they often don't have procedural self-talk. They tend to do the first few steps, then quit. Step sheets help them successfully do tasks—from start to finish.

STEP SHEET

STEPS	AMOUNT OF TIME
1.	
2.	
3.	
4.	
5.	
6.	
7.	
8.	
9.	
10.	
11.	
12.	

EXPLANATION

This activity is called a step sheet, a tool that helps students who ask what they should do even before you finish the directions for an assignment. Step sheets provide procedural information for academic tasks. If students cannot plan, they often don't have procedural self-talk. They tend to do the first few steps, then quit. Step sheets help them successfully do tasks on a consistent basis.

CLASSIFICATORY WRITING

Paragraph 1   INTRODUCTION
- 3+ sentences.
- Rewrite the prompt.
- Give general information and/or an opinion.

Paragraph 2   ADVANTAGES
- 8+ sentences.
- Make a statement: "There are advantages to ..."
- Write ADV 1 sentence.
- Elaborate using two sentences.
- Write ADV 2 sentence.
- Elaborate using two sentences.
- Make a concluding statement: "There are some advantages to ..."

Paragraph 3   ADVANTAGES OR DISADVANTAGES
- 8+ sentences.
- Make a statement: "Additionally, there are other advantages to ..." or "On the other hand, there are disadvantages to ..."
- Write ADV 3 or DIS 1 sentence.
- Elaborate using two sentences.
- Write ADV 4 or DIS 2 sentence.
- Elaborate using two sentences.
- Make a concluding statement.

Paragraph 4   DISADVANTAGES
- 8+ sentences.
- Make a statement.
- Write DIS 3 or DIS 1 sentence.
- Elaborate using two sentences.
- Write DIS 4 or DIS 2 sentence.
- Elaborate using two sentences.
- Make a concluding statement.

Paragraph 5   CONCLUSION
- 3+ sentences.
- Restate the prompt.
- Give specific information and/or opinions.

Developed by Molly Davis and Julie Heffner

EXPLANATION

This activity shows the students what each paragraph contains and how many paragraphs a piece of classificatory writing should have. This is another form of a step sheet because it provides procedural information for an academic task.

STRATEGY

ACADEMIC STRATEGIES	RESEARCHERS	EXPLANATION
Sketching for vocabulary	Apperly, I. A., Williams, E., and Williams, J. (2004). Marzano, R. (2007). Paquette, K. R., Fello, S. E., and Jalongo, M. R. (2007). Rohrer, T. (2006). Tanenhaus, M. K., Spivey-Knowlton, M. J., Eberhard, K. M., and Sedivy, J. C. (1995). Van Meter, P., Aleksic, M., Schwartz, A., and Garner, J. (2006).	Visual memory precedes verbal memory. Linguistic definitions were preceded by a visual representation in the brain.

SKETCHING FOR VOCABULARY

Divide a paper into two columns. Have the student write a word in the first column, then draw a picture (a visual representation of the word) in the second column. If the student cannot draw a visual representation of the word, he/she probably does not know the word. One of the fastest ways to teach vocabulary in any subject is to have students sketch. If they cannot sketch the word, they likely do not know it.

EXAMPLES OF SKETCHING

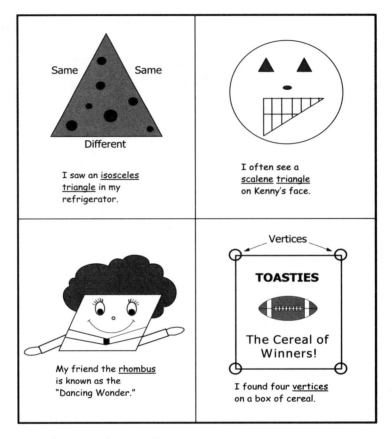

Adapted from materials by Cathy Fields

EXPLANATION

These are student examples of sketching activities using certain math terms: isosceles triangle, scalene triangle, rhombus, and vertices.

STRATEGY

10

ACADEMIC STRATEGIES	RESEARCHERS	EXPLANATION
Tucker signing strategy for decoding	Cole, C., and Majd, M. (2005) Thompson, R. L., Vinson, D. P., and Vigliocco, G. (2009).	The Center on Education and Lifelong Learning at Indiana University, in its evaluation of this decoding strategy, found the following growth: With the progress score being the difference between the number of words students could read on the pre- and post-tests, the mean progress score for the control group—no Tucker reading instruction—was only 5.30 points, as compared with 36.75 points for the experimental group. A student must be able to decode in order to comprehend. Decoding means that you know a symbol, e.g., *sh* represents a sound. This is a kinesthetic approach that uses both sides of the brain.

TUCKER SIGNING STRATEGY FOR DECODING

The Tucker Signing Strategies for Reading provide a kinesthetic method for translating between a sound and a symbol. In order to read, a person basically has to do two things: decode (the relationship between a sound and a symbol) and comprehend (make meaning). Tucker Signing has identified 44 sound chunks used in English. There is a hand movement for each sound chunk. When the student makes the movement, the movement translates a sound to an associated symbol.

MENTAL MODEL OF
MOVEMENT EXAMPLE

An effective movement mental model:
- Utilizes the least amount of movement necessary
- Is visible to and meaningful for the learner
- Contains no extraneous information

STRATEGY

ACADEMIC STRATEGIES	RESEARCHERS	EXPLANATION
Taking control of your own learning tools	Brink, J., Capps, E., and Sutko, A. (2004). Gladwell, M. (2008). Hoffman, A. (2003). Kirby, N. F., and Downs, C. T. (2007). Po-ying, C. (2007). Thompson, D. D., and McDonald, D. M. (2007).	Complexity, autonomy, and the relationship between effort and reward are the prerequisites for making meaning (Gladwell, 2008).

TAKING CONTROL OF YOUR OWN LEARNING TOOLS

The more clearly the expected end result is identified, the better the outcome and performance. Often guidance counselors do this at the secondary level, but it tends to be fairly perfunctory, given the demands on their time.

a. To help students pass the state assessment, a teacher did the following and was very successful. All of her students took a mock test in math. Then they scored their own papers. They made this grid:

Questions I got right and could get right again.	Questions I did or did not do correctly but am not sure how to do.	Questions where I had no clue.

In the top row, for each category, students wrote the numbers of the test questions and the objective it went with. Then they identified strategies that could be used with each objective. As they went through the questions, in the second row of boxes, they identified where they would put it, e.g., "no clue" got moved to "I know I could get it right."

We identified for students how many they had to get right to pass. The students then went back and counted how many questions were in each category and re-calculated what they thought their performance would be. Then they took another sample or mock test and refigured how they actually did. This is self-advocacy and provides tools for addressing a task.

STRATEGY

12

ACADEMIC STRATEGIES	RESEARCHERS	EXPLANATION
Self-assessment rubrics	Andrade, H. G. (1999a). Andrade, H. G. (1999b). Andrade, H. L., Du, Y., and Wang, X. (2008). Bloom, B. (1976). Bransford, J. D., Brown, A. L., and Cocking, R. R. (Eds.). (2000). Goddard, Y. L., and Sendi, C. (2008). Hafner, J. C., and Hafner, P. M. (2003). National Institute of Child Health and Human Development. (2000). Ross, J. A., and Starling, M. (2008).	Evaluation is at the highest level of Bloom's Taxonomy in thinking. It echoes Gladwell's comments above.

SELF-ASSESSMENT RUBRICS

At the top of Benjamin Bloom's chart of thinking skills is evaluation. To evaluate, a person must use criteria. To master your content area, you must know the criteria that indicate a skilled thinker in that area. The criteria tell you what is important and what is not important. When you provide rubrics for students to self-assess, they can then embed those criteria into learning.

RUBRIC TO MEASURE A SKILLED MUSICIAN (in Band and Orchestra)

CRITERIA	1	2	3	4
ACCURACY	Not in time Several wrong notes Wrong key	Mostly in correct time Misses notes Key is correct Fingerings are off	In correct time Mostly uses correct fingerings Notes are correct	Timing is virtually always correct Fingerings are correct Notes are virtually always correct
ARTICULATION	No variation in tempo Markings not observed No contrast in sound	Some variation in tempo but not correct Some contrast but incorrect for piece Random use of markings	Tempo mostly correct Mostly correct use of markings Dynamic contrast thin but correct	Markings are virtually always observed and followed Wide range of dynamic contrast Tempo is correct
SOUND QUALITY	Thin timbre High and low notes off Too loud or too soft for note or section Unpleasant to ear	Timbre for most notes is fuller All difficult notes have some timbre Use of sound markings is random	Timbre is mostly full Sound markings are used but not advantageously	Timbre is full Sound markings are correctly interpreted and followed
INTERPRETATION	No meaning assigned to piece No understanding of intent or purpose of composer	Playing indicates emotion but little understanding of meaning Understands that piece has climax but does not know where it is	Playing mostly conveys meaning and always conveys emotion Understands role of climax Can talk about intent and purpose	Playing conveys meaning and emotion Climax can be identified Plays truly to intent and purpose
ENSEMBLE CONTRIBUTION	Does not pay attention to conductor Listens only to his/her playing Too loud/too soft for group	Periodically pays attention to conductor Is mostly in balance with group Listens to his/her section Little understanding of his/her contribution to melody	Mostly follows conductor's interpretations In balance with group Mostly listens to piece as whole Can verbally articulate contribution to melody but does not always reflect that in his/her playing	Follows conductor's interpretation In balance with group Listens to piece as whole Understands his/her contribution to melody

EXPLANATION

An orchestra teacher and I wrote this to help his students better identify what a skilled musician would be. After a performance, the students highlight in one color what they think their performance was. The teacher highlights in another color what they think their performance was, after which the students make plans to address the discrepancy.

STRATEGY

13

ACADEMIC STRATEGIES	RESEARCHERS	EXPLANATION
Teaching another student	Andrade, H. G. (1999a). Andrade, H. G. (1999b). Andrade, H. L., Du, Y., and Wang, X. (2008). Bloom, B. (1976). Bransford, J. D., Brown, A. L., and Cocking, R. R. (Eds.). (2000). Goddard, Y. L., and Sendi, C. (2008). Hafner, J. C., and Hafner, P. M. (2003). National Institute of Child Health and Human Development. (2000). Ross, J. A., and Starling, M. (2008).	Brooks found that teaching another student yielded returns in achievement and resiliency.

TEACHING ANOTHER STUDENT

Teaching another student is a very powerful tool. When you can teach something successfully to someone else, you tend to understand it much better yourself.

STRATEGY

ACADEMIC STRATEGIES	RESEARCHERS	EXPLANATION
Planning academic tasks	Bakunas, B., and Holley, W. (2004). Bransford, J. D., Brown, A. L., and Cocking, R. R. (Eds.). (2000). Chalmers, D., and Lawrence, J. A. (1993). Collier, P. J., and Morgan, D. L. (2008). Feuerstein, R. (1980). Gambill, J. M., Moss, L. A., and Vescogni, C. D. (2008). Garcia-Ros, R., Perez-Gonzalez, F., and Hinojosa, E. (2004). Stoeger, H., and Ziegler, A. (2008). Yumusak, N., Sungur, S., and Cakiroglu, J. (2007).	To complete tasks requires planning, which requires procedural self-talk. Because the executive functions of some poor children's brains are less developed, planning and self-talk can be directly taught using games and procedural tools.

PLAN AND LABEL FOR ACADEMIC TASKS

There are at least four ways to systematically label tasks: numbering, lettering, assigning symbols, and color-coding. It is important to note that a systematic approach to the labeling means that fewer pieces of the task are skipped or missed.

For a task to be done correctly, a student must have:
- A plan
- A procedure
- Labels (vocabulary); labels are the tools the mind uses to address the task

There are several ways to teach this. It's easier to begin by using visual activities that have no words. This teaches students that all tasks must have a plan and labels.

PLAN AND LABEL IN MATH

1. 6⟌‾‾‾	Divisor: number of parts in a group
2. ⟌240	Dividend: total number of parts
3. ⟌⌢	Quotient: number of groups
4. 6⟌240	Are there enough parts for a group?
5. 6 ⟌240	Are there enough parts for a group? If so, how many groups?
6. × 4 6⟌24 ↳24	See if there are extra parts.

Source: Kim D. Ellis, *Putting the Pieces Together*

EXPLANATION

This is an example of plan and label as it pertains to division. Each of the six steps is an example of the plan and labels the students must be able to identify and follow to work through the steps of division.

One, two, and three (1–3) are the parts of the equation that the students should be able to identify and label. Four, five, and six (4–6) are the steps or the plan that the students need to follow to be able to work the division problem. These steps identify the questions/plan that the students must be able to answer/follow to solve the division equation.

STRATEGY

ACADEMIC STRATEGIES	RESEARCHERS	EXPLANATION
Planning your grade	Feuerstein, R. (1980).	To complete tasks requires planning, which requires procedural self-talk. Because the executive functions of some poor children's brains are less developed, planning and self-talk can be directly taught using games and procedural tools.

PLANNING YOUR GRADE

When you plan your grade, you are "keeping the end in mind." Planning controls impulsivity. In this particular example, when students plan their grade and review their current progress every Friday, they generally do much better academically.

ENGLISH III—MAKING THE GRADE

1. What work have I done well in my English class?
   a.
   b.
   c.
   d.

2. What work have I done poorly in my English class?
   a.
   b.
   c.
   d.

3. I was/was not satisfied with my grade in English III last semester.

   1st _____   2nd _____   3rd _____   Exam _____   Average _____

4. What grade do I realistically believe that I can earn this semester in English III?

5. What will I do in my English class to earn that grade?
   a.
   b.
   c.

EXPLANATION

At the beginning of the grading period, the teacher asks students to answer questions about the kinds of grades they want. Then each Friday the teacher gives 15 minutes for the students to record their grades from the week, calculate their averages, and identify what they must do to maintain or bring up their grades.

SPRING SEMESTER

Fourth Grading Period   I want to earn _____.

                              Daily 10%   Quiz 30%   Test 60%

Fifth Grading Period   I want to earn _____.

                              Daily 10%   Quiz 30%   Test 60%

Sixth Grading Period   I want to earn _____.

                              Daily 10%   Quiz 30%   Test 60%

I am/am not satisfied with my grade in English III this semester.

   1st _____   2nd _____   3rd _____   Exam _____   Average _____

EXPLANATION

This form is for students to use. It contains the percentage that daily work, quizzes, and tests count toward their quarterly grade. There is a place for them to record their actual grades.

STRATEGY

ACADEMIC STRATEGIES	RESEARCHERS	EXPLANATION
Translating casual register to formal register	Adger, C. (1994). Godley, A. J., and Minnici, A. (2008). Koch, L. M., Gross, A. M., and Kolts, R. (2001). Montano-Harmon, M. R. (1991). Olmedo, I. M. (2009). Wheeler, R. S. (2008).	To build formal register, one must use the current vocabulary and build upon it. One way to build it is to translate casual register (what is known—current schema) to formal register.

TRANSLATING CASUAL REGISTER TO FORMAL REGISTER

Formal register is the language used in school and work. It also is used in writing, and it's fairly specific. Casual register is the informal, even intimate, language between friends. To build formal register vocabulary, we ask students to translate from casual to formal register. For example, rather than saying, "She thinks she is all that," the student would say, "She thinks she is better than others."

STRATEGY

ACADEMIC STRATEGIES	RESEARCHERS	EXPLANATION
Writing organizers/text patterns	Chalk, J. C., Hagan-Burke, S., and Burke, M. D. (2005). Guastello, E. F., Beasley, T. M., and Sinatra, R. C., (2000). Idol, L., and Jones, B. F. (Eds.). (1991). Lin, H., and Chen. T. (2006). Mason, L. H., and Shriner, J. G. (2008). National Institute of Child Health and Human Development. (2000). Williams, J. P. (2005). Williams, J. P., Hall, K. M., and Lauer, K. D. (2004).	To write, one must organize against purpose for writing and structure of text. Teaching text patterns and organizers facilitates this process.

WRITING ORGANIZERS/TEXT PATTERNS

When comprehending text, the reader sorts the information either by the purpose for reading or the organizational structure of the text. By teaching K–12 students five basic patterns they will encounter in text, you are teaching them how to sort what is more important and less important in the text.

FIVE MODELS TO USE FOR SORTING

1. HAND

2. LADDER

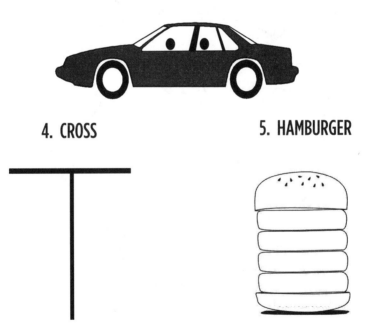

3. CAR

4. CROSS

5. HAMBURGER

EXPLANATION

Students will get much higher comprehension if they use one of the five techniques for sorting. In nonfiction there are basically five kinds of text. Each icon represents the five kinds of text and gives students a quick memory tool.

DESCRIPTIVE/TOPICAL

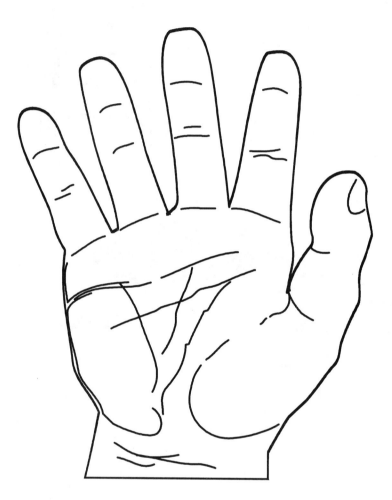

EXPLANATION

The hand is topical or descriptive. Use each finger to sort topics or descriptive details.

SEQUENCE/HOW-TO

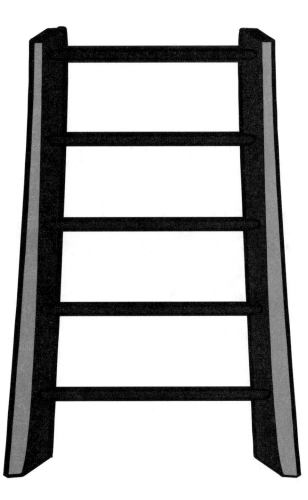

EXPLANATION

Label sequential steps on a ladder.

STORY STRUCTURE

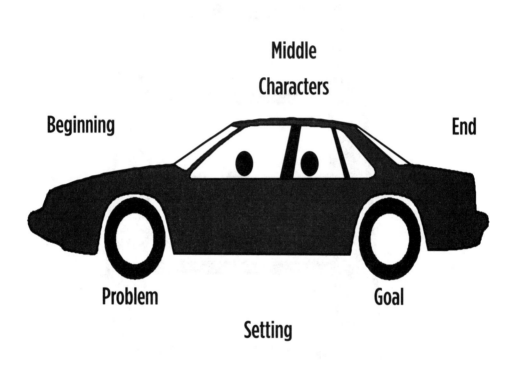

EXPLANATION

Use the car as a model to sort and remember. For example, in a piece of fiction there are characters, the beginning, the middle, the end, the episode, the problem, the goal, and the setting.

COMPARE/CONTRAST
ADVANTAGES/DISADVANTAGES
CAUSE/EFFECT

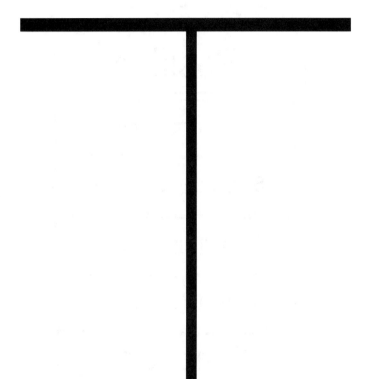

EXPLANATION

Use the two sides of the T-shape to compare and contrast.

PERSUASIVE REASONS

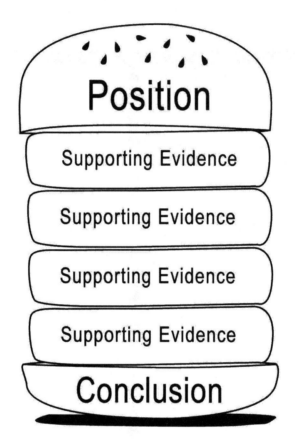

EXPLANATION

If you use a hamburger, the top bun represents the person's position. Each layer in the sandwich is a piece of supporting evidence. The bottom bun is the conclusion.

STRATEGY

18

ACADEMIC STRATEGIES	RESEARCHERS	EXPLANATION
Relational learning	Domagala-Zysk, E. (2006).	Relational learning involves seven characteristics. See Payne (2008).
	Faircloth, B. S., and Hamm, J. V. (2005).	
	Good, M., and Adams, G. R. (2008).	
	Green, G., Rhodes, J., Hirsch, A. H., Suarez-Orozco, C., and Camic, P. M. (2008).	
	Guay, F., Marsh, H. W., Senecal, C., and Dowson, M. (2008).	
	Johnson, Lisa S. (2008).	
	Payne, R. K. (2008).	
	Putnam, R. (2000).	
	Reis, S. M., Colbert, R. D., and Hebert, T. P. (2005).	
	Rimm-Kaufman, S. E., and Chiu, Y.-J. I. (2007).	
	Ross, D. D., Bondy, E., Gallingane, C., and Hambacher, E. (2008).	
	Sanchez, B., Reyes, O., and Singh, J. (2006).	
	Scales, P. C., Benson, P. L., Roehlkepartain, E. C., Sesma, A., Jr., and van Dulmen, M. (2006).	

WHAT IS RELATIONAL LEARNING?

Relational learning involves seven characteristics:

1. Relationships of mutual respect with teachers and administrators
2. A peer group to belong to that is positive and not destructive
3. A coach or advocate who helps the student
4. If not a member of the dominant culture, the student has access to individuals (or histories of individuals) who have attained success and retained connections to their roots
5. Bridging social capital * (e-mail buddies, mentors, et al.) to the larger society
6. At the secondary level, a very specific and clear plan for addressing his/her own learning performance
7. A safe environment (emotionally, verbally, and physically)

* **Social capital** is terminology used by Robert Putnam in his book *Bowling Alone*. It basically means who you know. He identifies two kinds—bonding and bridging. **Bonding** social capital involves people who are like you; **bridging** social capital involves people different from you.

Relational Learning Frame		
Subject Area/Content: Teacher provides structure for academic connectedness	**Social Context:** Teacher provides structure for social connectedness	**Teacher/School as Coach:** Teacher/school provides structure for personal connectedness
■ Content frames ■ Future story ■ Mental models ■ Question making skills ■ Step sheets ■ Study skill sheets ■ Test preparation	■ Classroom atmosphere ■ Classroom interactions ■ Hidden rules ■ Positive peer group ■ Positive physical regard ■ Rapport/respect ■ Registers of language ■ Student interests	■ Connecting future story with school goals ■ Emotional objectivity ■ Evaluating content performance vs. social performance ■ Feedback and praise ■ Generation Y: Who are they? ■ Personal attention ■ Plan for a grade

Developed by Guy Todnem

STRATEGY

19

ACADEMIC STRATEGIES	RESEARCHERS	EXPLANATION
Structured partners in learning	Bransford, J. D., Brown, A. L., and Cocking, R. R. (Eds.). (2000). Cheung, A., and Slavin, R. E. (2005). Galton, M., Hargreaves, L., and Pell, T. (2009). Gillies, R. M. (2004). Gillies, R. M. (2008). Mahalingam, M., Schaefer, F., and Morlino, E. (2008). National Institute of Child Health and Human Development. (2000).	Talking opens neural pathways, builds relationships, and enhances understandings.

STRUCTURED PARTNERS IN LEARNING

Having structured partners in learning helps students dialogue about the learning and opens neural pathways. Paired reading, working with a partner, thinking aloud, etc., are all ways to accomplish this intervention.

STRATEGY

ACADEMIC STRATEGIES	RESEARCHERS	EXPLANATION
Mental models for processes	Bransford, J. D., Brown, A. L., and Cocking, R. R. (Eds.). (2000). Bruner, J. (2006). Committee on the Support for Thinking Spatially. (2006). Idol, L., and Jones, B. F. (1991). Jones, B. F., Pierce, J., and Hunter, B. (1988). Marzano, R. (2007). Marzano, R., and Arrendondo, D. (1986). Payne, R. K. (2005). Payne, R. K. (2007). Resnick, L., and Klopfer, L. (1989). Senge, P. (1994). Shulman, L. (1987).	Visual representation is one of the areas in which poor and affluent brains are no different. Many studies indicate that mental models enhance learning. Bruner (2006) stated that all learning involves task and context.

MENTAL MODELS FOR PROCESSES

Mental models translate an abstract task to a concrete reality. Not only does the brain have to do this for content, it also must do so for processes.

MENTAL MODEL FOR PLAN AND LABEL:
MATH PROBLEM-SOLVING QTIPS

Plan and Label—QTIPS
Math Problem-Solving
Math Problem Solving

Letter	Step	Teacher Directions	Symbol	Sentence Starter
Q	Question	Use sentence frame to underline question		I was asked to ...
T	Think	Thoughtfully, thoroughly, and totally read problem		
I	Information	Circle important information and labels; cross out unnecessary information		I knew ...
P	Plan	Choose plan, operation, or strategy: OPERATION STRATEGY STEPS		I used ...
S	Solution	Show your work; choose your answer; check your answer	X = 10	The answer is ... because ...

Lodi Unified Schools, Morada Middle School, Stockton, CA, 2004–05

EXPLANATION

This is another process for math problem solving.

MENTAL MODEL FOR RESPONDING TO OPEN-RESPONSE QUESTIONS: U R TOPS

U	UNDERLINE	UNDERLINE or highlight key words, ideas, power verbs, and important information.
R	READ	READ everything twice before you start to answer. Read charts, diagrams, and maps, then reread the question.
T	TOPIC	Create a TOPIC SENTENCE that clearly states your position, decision, or starts your answer.
O	ORGANIZE	ORGANIZE your thoughts to answer the question. Be clear, concise, and to the point.
P	PART	Look for specific PARTS to be answered. Label each part with a number.
S	SUPPORT	SUPPORT your answer with facts, figures, or statements from what is given.

Source: Kim D. Ellis, *Putting the Pieces Together*

EXPLANATION

Step sheet:

Study the mental model to determine the meaning of each step of the U R TOPS process.

Follow each step of the mental model to answer Open-Response Questions.

Put a check over the letters of the U R TOPS steps as you complete them.

Write your response.

STRATEGY

21

ACADEMIC STRATEGIES	RESEARCHERS	EXPLANATION
Sorting important from unimportant using summarizing, cartooning, graphic organizers, visuals, compare/contrast activities	Guastello, E. F., Beasley, T. M., and Sinatra, R. C. (2000). Hagaman, J. L., and Reid, R. (2008). Hock, M., and Mellard, D. (2005). Kirkpatrick, L. C., and Klein, P. D. (2009). Langford, P. A., Rizzo, S. K., and Roth, J. M. (2003). Marzano, R. (2007). Reiner, M. (2009). Richards, J. C., and Anderson, N. A. (2003). Tanenhaus, M. K., Spivey-Knowlton, M. J., Eberhard, K. M., and Sedivy, J. C. (1995). van der Schoot, M., Vasbinder, A. L., Horsley, T. M., and van Lieshout, E. C. D. M. (2008). Weekes, H. (2005).	Memory is based upon summarization and/or attachment to prior knowledge. Summarization is based upon sorting important from unimportant. To sort what is and is not important, one must identify similarities and differences (compare and contrast).

SORTING INFORMATION USING PATTERNS AND CRITERIA

To store and retrieve information, one must be able to sort using criteria. If the patterns are known, however, one can sort faster. Because children from poverty often come into school behind, ways are needed to teach information much faster. Teaching patterns as a way to sort is one way to shorten the time needed to teach something.

The mind sorts data against patterns, mental mindsets, and paradigms to determine what is "important" and what is not.

Items with the same attributes are assigned to a group.

Patterns can be identified using groups.

Abstract constructs are essential for grouping and patterning; these are necessary for success in school.

DEVELOPING SORTING STRATEGIES

The mind sorts data against patterns, mental mindsets, and paradigms to determine what is "important" and what is not.

Attributes become a sort of screen that allows "important" data to continue and stops "unimportant" data.

By teaching patterns within data, students can find what is "important" more quickly and accurately.

IDENTIFYING CHARACTERISTICS

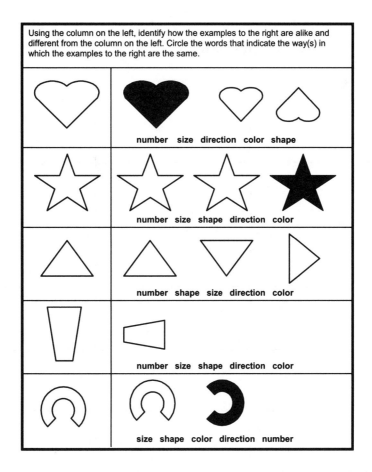

EXPLANATION

Using the column on the left, identify how the examples to the right are alike and different from the column on the left. Circle the words that indicate the way(s) in which the examples to the right are the same.

117

IDENTIFYING CHARACTERISTICS:
WORDS—ALIKE AND DIFFERENT

In the first column, write what the words have in common. In the second column, write how the words are different.

Words	Alike	Different
Sugar **Salt**		
Day **Night**		
Paper **Pencil**		
Car **Truck**		
Now **Later**		
Here **There**		
Tall **Short**		

EXPLANATION

In the first column write what the words have in common. In the second column write how the words are different.

SORTING BY CRITERIA AND PATTERNS

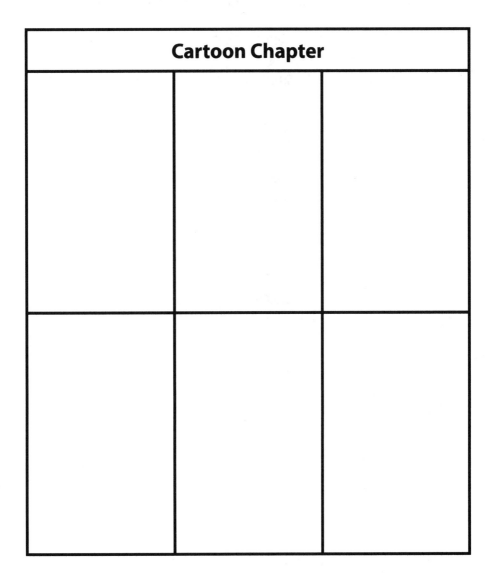

EXPLANATION

Have students use this activity to draw their own cartoon characters or have them cut out cartoon characters they find in the newspaper. Have the students sort them using criteria and patterns that they develop through their drawings or through the characters they choose to cut out and paste in the squares.

TO SORT, THE MIND USES PATTERNS AND CRITERIA (ATTRIBUTES)

Criteria may be:

structure
purpose
number
size
direction
color
shape
detail
type
pattern
function
design

STRATEGY

22

ACADEMIC STRATEGIES	RESEARCHERS	EXPLANATION
Fiction reading organizer/sorter	Conlon, T. (2009). Idol, L., and Jones, B. F. (1991). Jones, B. F., Pierce, J., and Hunter, B. (1988). National Institute of Child Health and Human Development. (2000). Stone, R. H., Boon, R. T., Fore, C., III, Bender, W. N., and Spencer, V. G. (2008).	To summarize fiction, one has to remember the characters; the beginning, middle, and end (plot development); the setting; and the problem and/or goal. Any organizer that helps a student identify these things facilitates summarization and sorting.

FICTION READING ORGANIZER/SORTER

Fiction requires the writer to have a beginning, a middle, and an end; a setting; characters; a problem; and a goal. If readers can identify those elements in a story, then they can comprehend the story.

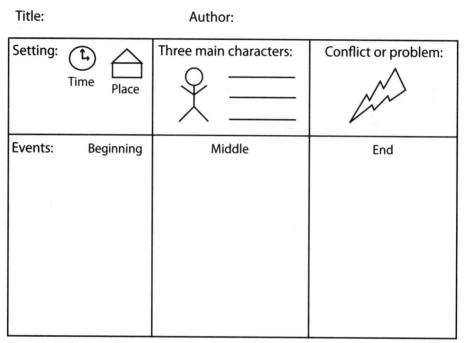

Source: Kim D. Ellis, *Putting the Pieces Together*

EXPLANATION

Students complete each box with the information from the story.

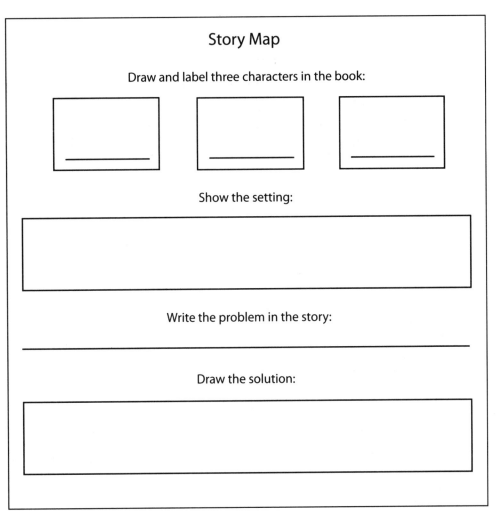

Source: Kim D. Ellis, *Putting the Pieces Together*

EXPLANATION

Another organizer to sort what is important to remember in a story.

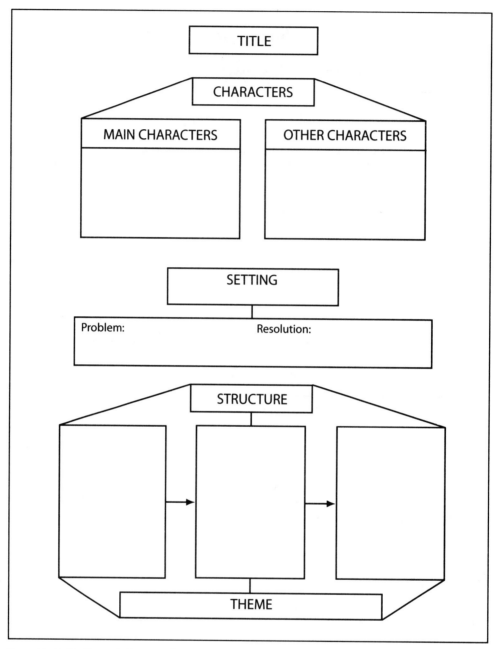

Source: Kim D. Ellis, *Putting the Pieces Together*

EXPLANATION

Another organizer to sort what is important in a story.

STORY PLOT CHART

Title:
Author:
Setting:
> **Time:**
> **Place:**
> **General:**
> **Specific:**

Problem or goal:

Circle one:

MAN against MAN   **MAN against NATURE**   **MAN against SELF**

Events:
> 1.
> 2.
> 3.
> 4.
> 5.

Event that solved the problem:

Message of theme:

Source: Kim D. Ellis, *Putting the Pieces Together*

EXPLANATION

Another organizer to sort what is important in a story.

STRATEGY

ACADEMIC STRATEGIES	RESEARCHERS	EXPLANATION
Envelope system for research papers and reports	Ellis, K. D. (2004).	Models are necessary for the systematic gathering of data. The envelope system is for the facilitation of part to whole of tasks. Twenty percent of the grade is based upon using the process. Eighty percent of the grade is based on the final report.

ENVELOPE SYSTEM FOR RESEARCH PAPERS AND REPORTS

The process of research requires than an individual pull information from multiple sources. Because this is an abstract task, many students have difficulty with it. The method of using envelopes to collect research (in relation to topics and sources) helps students understand the process and complete it effectively.

MENTAL MODEL FOR PART TO WHOLE

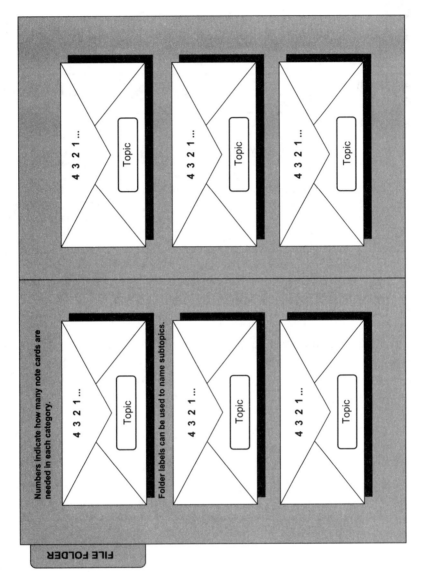

Source: Kim D. Ellis, *Putting the Pieces Together*

EXPLANATION

Have students take a manila folder and glue six envelopes onto the inside of it with the flaps on the outside. This helps them visually see part to whole, especially when they have to divide a report into parts. When you first teach this you may need to give them some of the groupings, but after two or three times they can figure it out.

STRATEGY

ACADEMIC STRATEGIES	RESEARCHERS	EXPLANATION
Language/vocabulary development	Carrell, C. (1987). Joshi, R. M. (2005). Tanenhaus, M. K., Spivey-Knowlton, M. J., Eberhard, K. M., and Sedivy, J. C. (1995).	Vocabulary is the tool the brain uses to think. Formal register is the vocabulary or ideas and abstract representational systems. Playful, relational, associative activities build vocabulary, as well as sketching.

VOCABULARY DEVELOPMENT

Vocabulary development is essential to thinking and shared understandings. Vocabulary is developed in part by knowing how things are alike and how they are different. It's easier to identify differences than it is to identify similarities. Here are two strategies for vocabulary development.

#1 KNOWLEDGE RATINGS

Using a graph like the one below, have students list the words in the first column to be studied. They evaluate their knowledge level of each word and check the appropriate box. If they have some idea of the meaning, they write in their guess. Following discussion or study, they write the definition in their own words. This activity is particularly useful in helping students develop metacognitive (being able to think about one's own thinking) awareness.

Example:

WORD	Know	Think I know	Have heard	GUESS	DEFINITION
saline			X	A liquid for contact lenses	A salt solution

Activity:

WORD	Know	Think I know	Have heard	GUESS	DEFINITION
torsade					
lurdane					
macula					

#2 WORD DANGLES

Students read a novel or story and then, on a piece of construction paper, illustrate it and write a summary of it. From the selection, they choose approximately five words that interest them, then write and illustrate each word on a separate card. They write a definition of the word on the reverse side of the card. The cards subsequently are attached to the bottom of the construction paper and "dangle" from it. The finished product can be hung as a mobile.

By using "word dangles," students enhance their comprehension. The illustrations also help them with conceptualization. They learn how vocabulary, reading, and writing are connected. The strategy is adaptable for all content areas, including fine arts. For example, in math, students might write a summary of a process and write, define, and illustrate several key words for that process. "Word dangles" also provide a word-rich environment and stimulate student interest in vocabulary study.

Example:

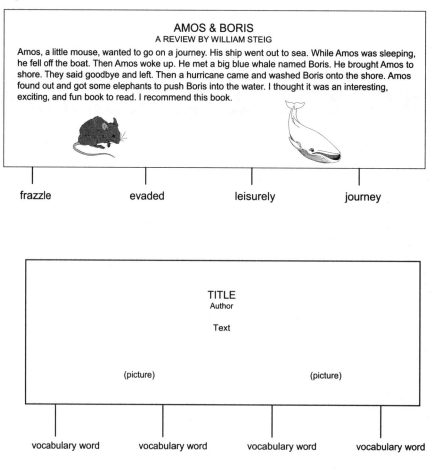

#3 PICTURE IT

With each new story/reading, assign each student one vocabulary word. Students must:

- Find the word in the story/reading and record the page number (see form below).
- Find the word in the dictionary and record the pronunciation, number of syllables, part of speech, and definition used in the story.
- Create a picture of the word (on the second form below) to represent the word.
- Present the word to the class using the definition and picture.

Activity:

_____	_____
(word)	(page number)
_____ _____ _____	
(pronunciation) (# of syllables) (part of speech)	
Definition from story_____	
_____	
_____	

Word picture

#4 WORD WEB

Students write the target word in the box, then write a synonym, an antonym, a definition, and an experience to complete the web.

Example:

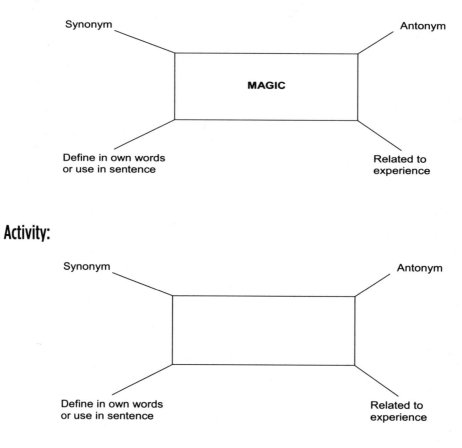

Activity:

#5 CONCEPT BUILDING

Guessing opposites or seeing relationships:

To a small group, the teacher says:
1.   Candy is sweet, but pickles are _____
2.   An airplane is fast, but a horse is _____
3.   The sky is above; the ground is _____

This type of procedure can also be used to elicit analogies.

Examples:

1.   Pies are made by a baker; clothes are made by a _____
2.   A cat runs on its legs, but a car runs on _____
3.   In the morning the sun rises; at night the sun _____

The level at which this exercise can be done will vary widely with different children.

Activity:

1.   _____
2.   _____
3.   _____

#6 INTERMEDIATE ADAPTATION

With each text reading, assign each student one vocabulary word. Students must do the following:

- Find the word in the text.
- Copy text definition (taken directly from book).
- Write own definition (in student's own words).
- Use discriminating/distinguishing characteristics (information that helps to give more details about the word).
- Draw illustration (drawing that gives a visual representation of the word).

Example:

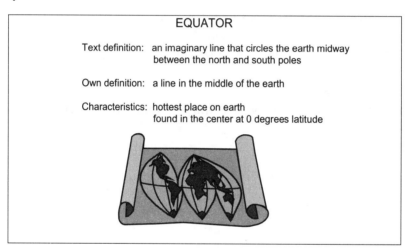

EQUATOR

Text definition: an imaginary line that circles the earth midway
between the north and south poles

Own definition: a line in the middle of the earth

Characteristics: hottest place on earth
found in the center at 0 degrees latitude

Activity:

Materials needed: text reading, vocabulary list, teacher-developed worksheet

Vocabulary Word Map

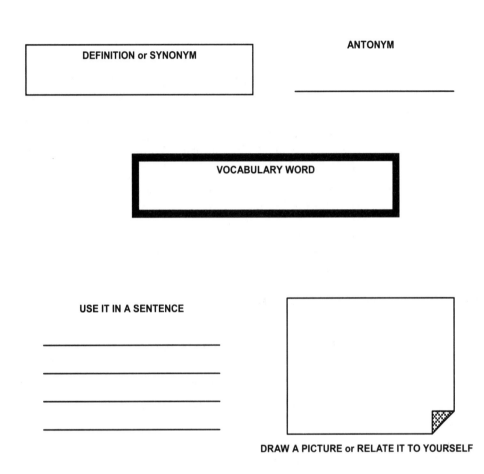

DEFINITION or SYNONYM

ANTONYM
_____

VOCABULARY WORD

USE IT IN A SENTENCE

_____

_____

_____

_____

DRAW A PICTURE or RELATE IT TO YOURSELF

Adapted from materials of Raymond C. Jones, found at www.readingquest.org

EXPLANATION

Have the students write a vocabulary word in the box in the middle of the page under the vocabulary word. Then have the students write the definition or synonym for the word in the box for definition or synonym. Have the student then write on the line an antonym for the word. Next the students should be able to use the word in a sentence. Finally, have the students sketch a mental model for the word. If the word is love, they might draw a heart. If the word is religion, they might draw a cross or a church.

STRATEGY

ACADEMIC STRATEGIES	RESEARCHERS	EXPLANATION
Teaching input strategies using games	Gredler, M. E. (2004). Kishiyama, M. M., Boyce, W. T., Jimenez, A. M., Perry L. M., and Knight, R. T. (2008). Leemkuil, H., Jong, T. D., and Ootes, S. (2000). Rieber, L. P. (2005).	See chart on pages 138–139 of this book for games that can be used. Input strategies help one gather data. Games are relational and competitive, and they build many of these skills.

TEACHING INPUT STRATEGIES USING GAMES

Input strategies are the methods by which the brain gathers data. To put it in obvious terms, data must be in the brain before information can be useful. In EEG scans done at the University of California, Berkeley (2008), researchers found that most children from poverty have not developed the prefrontal cortex (executive function) of the brain in the way that most middle-class children have. The executive function of the brain is impulse control, working memory (holding one idea while you work with another), organization and planning. Games help one do these things.

COGNITIVE STRATEGIES

INPUT: Quantity and quality of data gathered

1. Use planning behaviors.
2. Focus perception on specific stimulus.
3. Control impulsivity.
4. Explore data systematically.
5. Use appropriate and accurate labels.
6. Organize space using stable systems of reference.
7. Orient data in time.
8. Identify constancies across variations.
9. Gather precise and accurate data.
10. Consider two sources of information at once.
11. Organize data (parts of a whole.)
12. Visually transport data.

ELABORATION: Efficient use of the data

1. Identify and define the problem.
2. Select relevant cues.
3. Compare data.
4. Select appropriate categories of time.
5. Summarize data.
6. Project relationship of data.
7. Use logical data.
8. Test hypothesis.
9. Build inferences.
10. Make a plan using the data.
11. Use appropriate labels.
12. Use data systematically.

OUTPUT: Communication of elaboration and input

1. Communicate clearly the labels and processes.
2. Visually transport data correctly.
3. Use precise and accurate language.
4. Control impulsive behavior.

Adapted from work of Reuven Feuerstein

INPUT PROCESS SKILLS

Skill	Definition	How does the lack of process impact class-room performance?	Games/activities that will strengthen this process
Uses planning behaviors	Goal setting, identifying proce-dures in task, assigning time to task, and identifying quality of work necessary for task	Does not turn homework in on time, unable to com-plete long-term projects, cause/effect (if I do this, then this will happen), sequence, impulsivity	Logic puzzles, Set, chess
Focuses perception on specific stimulus	Strategy of seeing details and identifying everything noticed by five senses	Cannot focus on assigned task, misses parts of task, cannot find information on page	Any board game, knit-ting, crochet, sequential strategies (checklists)
Controls impulsivity	Strategy of stopping action until one has thought about task	Cannot plan, gets in trouble, may be misdiag-nosed as having ADHD, finishes assignments too quickly	Any board game
Explores data systematically	Strategy of procedurally and systematically going through every piece of data	Cannot see patterns, relationships between data; does not have method for checking work	Jigsaw puzzles, Set, using highlighter to find important pieces of information
Uses appropriate and accurate labels	Precise use of words to identify and explain	Uses generic words instead of specific ones, cannot do "Cloze" procedure tests	Create mental models of new vocabulary
Organizes space with stable systems of reference	Can identify with words in position of an item, can organize space	Disorganized, misplaces things, mixes up *b, d, p, q* (mimics dyslexia), cannot read map, cannot line up numbers in math	Jigsaw puzzles, 9-square puzzles, counted cross-stitch
Orients data in time	Strategy of assigning abstract values to time and use of measurements of time	Cannot sequence, loses track of time, does not turn things in on time	Comic strip activities, sequence, using timer
Identifies constancies across variations	Strategy of knowing what always remains the same and what changes	Cannot see patterns, can-not make generalizations, cannot find main idea, cannot compare/contrast	Jigsaw puzzles, Set, attribute trains

Skill	Definition	How does the lack of process impact classroom performance?	Games/activities that will strengthen this process
Gathers precise and accurate information	Strategy of using specific vocabulary and word choice, identifying precisely when something occurred in space	Cannot summarize because cannot distinguish between what's important and what's not; cannot tell *where, when, how*	Highlighters or highlighting tape, *I Spy* books
Considers two pieces of information at once	Strategy of mind holding two objects simultaneously and comparing/contrasting the two objects	Cannot compare/contrast, find patterns	1-2-3 Oy!, counted cross-stitch, plastic canvas
Organizes data (parts of a whole)	Strategy of going through data systematically, organizing space, identifying constancies and variations, and using vocabulary to label both parts and whole	Cannot explain why, does not recognize when someone is cheating	Jigsaw puzzles
Visually transports data	Strategy of eye picking up data, then carrying it accurately into brain, examining it for constancies and variations, and labeling parts and whole	Cannot copy from blackboard or overhead, colors in wrong answers on Scantron	Feuerstein's dot puzzles, any activity where students must follow pattern

Developed by Karen Jensen; adapted with permission

STRATEGY

ACADEMIC STRATEGIES	RESEARCHERS	EXPLANATION
Spatial orientation/ transferring objects in representational space	Committee on the Support for Thinking Spatially. (2006). Feuerstein, R. (1980). Gunzelmann, G. (2008). Gyselinck, V., Meneghetti, C., De Beni, R., and Pazzaglia, F. (2009).	Needed for organization and math (rotate this object). Spatial orientation is how objects are represented in space, e.g., a map represents objects in space.

SPATIAL ORIENTATION/TRANSFERRING OBJECTS IN REPRESENTATIONAL SPACE

Spatial orientation or transferring objects in representational space is a critical skill for reading maps, doing math (*up, down, across, over*), reading (difference between *b, d, p, q*), etc. Three-dimensional objects don't look the same on paper as two-dimensional items. Students must be taught how what is on paper or computer represents it in real life, i.e., a map represents objects in space.

MENTAL MODEL FOR SPACE

On which side of the tip of the arrow is the dot?

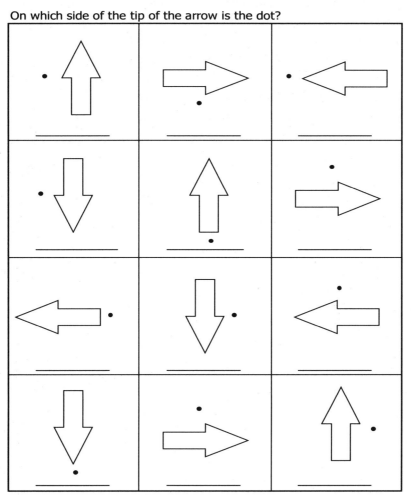

Source: Kim D. Ellis, *Putting the Pieces Together*

EXPLANATION

Mental model for space: This is one way in which we diagnose, ascertain, and teach space.

Stand up and put the end of your pencil or pen on the end of your nose like this. Face me. The tip of your pencil is the tip of the arrow. This dot is your arm. Now the question is as follows: To which side of the tip of the arrow is the dot? And the answer to your first box (upper-left-hand corner) is left.

This is called directionality. If you cannot do this, you have serious problems in math and problems on IQ tests.

This is exactly how we teach directionality and get it inside students' heads. We say to them, "You know, inside your head you're holding information, and when your eyes go up, it helps you get the pictures that you have inside your head and put them in there … We are going to do this inside your head—get the picture in here."

Students cannot be neat unless you give them a representational system to carry in their heads. As an example help students develop a map of their desk. This is an abstract representation, students cannot find things without it.

PLAN AND LABEL SPACE

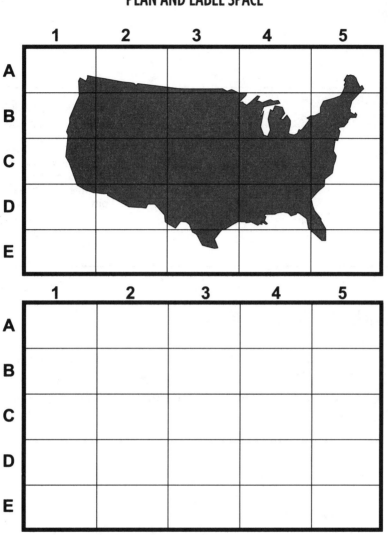

Source: Kim D. Ellis, *Putting the Pieces Together*

EXPLANATION

The map shown represents the shape of the contiguous United States. This map is solid and focuses on the outline, but other maps could be used to illustrate states and physical features.

Have students select a box from the top grid and count to locate the exact box in the grid below. Students should then replicate the boundary line in the new box, ultimately connecting the boundary line all the way around the map.

143

STRATEGY

ACADEMIC STRATEGIES	RESEARCHERS	EXPLANATION
Teaching adverbs and prepositions	Payne, R. K. (2005).	Very few adverbs or prepositions are used in casual register. Prepositions and adverbs are needed for math, physical education, and social studies, e.g., *up, down, over, under, left, right.*

TEACHING ADVERBS AND PREPOSITIONS

Casual register does not use many adverbs or prepositions. Prepositions and adverbs (*up, down, over, under, left, right,* etc.) are all used extensively in reading maps, doing math, etc. Prepositions and adverbs can be directly taught in physical education in particular as a way to enhance academics.

ACADEMIC STRATEGIES	RESEARCHERS	EXPLANATION
Eyes in the visual position	Andreas, F. (1994). Buckner, M., Meara, N. M., Reese, E. J., and Reese, M. (1987).	Neurologically, when eyes are up, the brain is accessing visual information. Important for math.

RELATIONSHIP OF EYE MOVEMENT TO PROCESSING

Eye movement is neurologically related to brain processing. When the eyes are up, the brain is accessing visual information. We ask students to put their eyes up so that they can access what is stored visually. On math tests, when it says to rotate those figures in your head … this requires the eyes to be in the visual position.

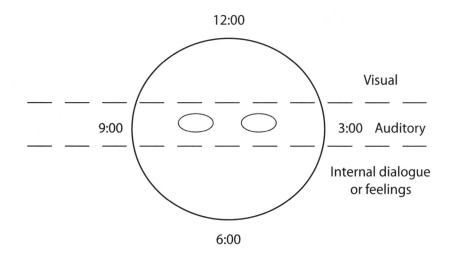

STRATEGY

ACADEMIC STRATEGIES	RESEARCHERS	EXPLANATION
Mental model for formal register	Bruce, C., Snodgrass, D., and Salzman, J. A. (1999). Greene, V., and Enfield, M. (1967). Schacter, J. (2001). *Success Stories/Evidence Data.* (2006). Swan, W. (2007). Wolff, J. (2002). www.ahaprocess.com/ files/R&D_School/PSM ResearchSummary _2004-2006.pdf	Writing fluency is based upon formal register. This mental model from Project Read enhances fluency and sentence composition. Swan's research data on our work indicate that if the mental model is used consistently, it results in extraordinary writing scores.

MENTAL MODEL FOR FORMAL REGISTER

Writing in formal register is required for work and school. The writing prompts on state assessments require the use of formal register. Formal register follows a pattern. This mental model teaches the basic patterns.

MENTAL MODEL FOR FORMAL REGISTER—WRITTEN EXPRESSION

Sentence Frame

Reminds me that a sentence must have a capital letter at the beginning and a stop sign
at the end. The effect of the sentence is expressed by the question mark (?) above the
period or the exclamation point (!) above the period.

? . !

Bare-Bones Sentence

Teri danced.

A sentence must contain a subject and a predicate. The predicate can be an action predicate word.
Example: Teri danced.

Or the predicate can be a bound predicate.
Example: Teri is dancing.

The subject names a *person*, *place*, *thing*, or *idea*.

The action predicate expresses physical or mental action such as the following examples.

moved   kicked   thought   imagined

Predicate Expanders

The predicate can be expanded by expressing the   how   when   where   why   of the action.

Example:

how   where   when

The waves pounded   relentlessly   against the small boat   as the fisherman struggled to reach shore   .

Predicate Expanders:

How	=	degree	adverbs (-ly ending, like or as, with/without)
When	=	time	before, during, after, when, while, since
Where	=	position	prepositional phrases (to, from, against, behind)
Why	=	reason	because, to, so, for

Subject Describer

Words that describe physical characteristics, personality, numbers, and ownership.

Source: Project Read® excerpt reprinted with permission of copyright holder, LanguageCircle Enterprises, Inc., and
its creators Victoria Greene and Mary Lee Enfield, Ph.D. Contact: (800) 450-0343. www.projectread.com

EXPLANATION

This mental model is for formal register. A sentence starts with a capital letter and ends
with a punctuation mark. It has a subject and a verb. A straight line is the subject, and
a wavy line is the verb. A rectangle describes the subject, and a triangle expands the
verb. A triangle answers one of four questions: *how, when, where,* or *why.*

STRATEGY

ACADEMIC STRATEGIES	RESEARCHERS	EXPLANATION
Plan and label	"Annotated Bibliography of MLE, LPAD, & IE, 1990–2005 (including Selected Bibliography of Prof. R. Feuerstein)." (2006). "Mediated Learning Experience in Teaching and Counseling—Proceedings of the International Conferences 'Models of Teaching Training' and 'Educational Advancement for Youth at Risk.'" (2001). Ben-Hur, M. (Ed.). (1994). Feuerstein, R. (1998). Feuerstein, R., et al. (2003). Feuerstein, R., Klein, P., and Tannenbaum, A. (Eds.). (1991). Feuerstein, R., Mintzker, Y., Ben-Shachar, N., and Cohen, M. (2001). Feuerstein, R., Rand, Y., and Feuerstein, R. S. (2006). Feuerstein, R., Rand, Y., Falik, L., and Feuerstein, R. S. (2003). Feuerstein, R., Rand, Y., Falik, L., and Feuerstein, R. S. (2006). Feuerstein, S. (2002). Howie, D. R. (2003). Kozulin, A. (2001). Kozulin, A. (Ed.). (1997). Kozulin, A., and Rand, Y. (Eds.). (2000).	Payne's work combines content comprehension and Feuerstein's work on processes. The student can use the vocabulary of the task and can proceduralize the process to get the task done.

ACADEMIC STRATEGIES	RESEARCHERS	EXPLANATION
Plan and label (continued)	Lebeer, J. (Ed.). (2003). Mohan, B., and Slater, T. (2006). Payne, R. K. (2005). Seok-Hoon Seng, A., Kwee-Hoon Pou, L., Oon-Seng Tan (Eds.). (2003). Watson, S., and Miller, T. (2009). Woodward-Kron, R. (2008).	

PLAN AND LABEL

Payne's work combines content comprehension and Feuerstein's work on processes.

The student can use the vocabulary of the task and can proceduralize the process to get the task done.

To do any task a person must have language and a process. Planning provides the process. Labeling provides the language.

PLAN AND LABEL IN SCIENCE

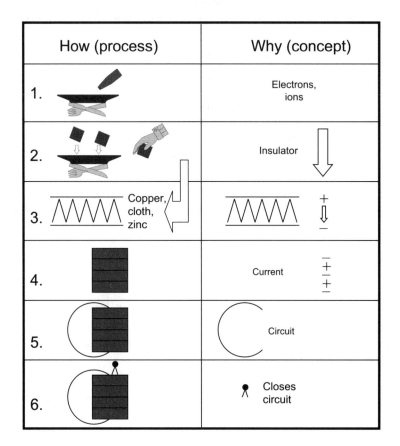

How (process)	Why (concept)
1.	Electrons, ions
2.	Insulator
3. Copper, cloth, zinc	+ −
4.	Current + + +
5.	Circuit
6.	Closes circuit

EXPLANATION

This is a process/concept chart. The student tells what is done and explains how.

Step 1: The vinegar is poured into a dish. Why? … *Because it provides electrons and ions.*

Step 2: Pieces of cloth are dipped into vinegar. Why? ... *Because it provides a conductor and insulator.*

Step 3: The cloth is placed between pieces of copper and zinc. Why? ... *Because they give and take electrons.*

Step 4: There are four stacks of cloth, zinc, and copper. Why do we need to stack four? ... *Because it makes a current.*

Step 5: Aluminum foil connects the top and bottom of the stack.

Step 6: A light is placed at the top. Why? ... *To close the circuit.*

STRATEGY

31

ACADEMIC STRATEGIES	RESEARCHERS	EXPLANATION
Automaticity	Bloom, B. (1976).	The more complex a process, the more parts of that process have to be automatic. Math facts are an example. In reading, you have to decode at a rate that does not interfere with learning. Sports coaches know that automaticity—the ability to respond automatically—is critical to success. Automaticity requires practice.

STRATEGY

BEHAVIORAL STRATEGIES

BEHAVIORAL STRATEGIES	RESEARCHERS	EXPLANATION
Self-assessment of resources	Devol, P. E. (2004). DeWitz, S. J., Woolsey, M. L., and Walsh, W. B. (2009). Krebs, C. (2006). Vickerstaff, S., Heriot, S., Wong, M., Lopes, A., and Dossetor, D. (2007).	Response to any environment is the ability to name it. When one knows one's own resource base, resources can be leveraged because they can be named.

WHY LOOK AT RESOURCES?

It isn't possible to educate well just by teaching the "group" and not knowing about the individual students in the classroom. Many students get identified as "at risk" when the issue is one of resources. When you know the resources of an individual, then you can determine the intervention(s) that will work best. Interventions that are successful work with the individual's strengths to enhance his/her under-developed resources.

WHAT DOES IT MEAN TO BE UNDER-RESOURCED? IS IT A PERSONAL ISSUE OR A SITUATIONAL ISSUE?

It is both. All individuals have an area or areas in their life where they would like to have more resources, i.e., more athletic abilities and better eyesight—or be taller, shorter, smarter, quicker, etc.

Under-resourced is defined as not having the resources to address a particular situation or negotiate a particular environment.

All resources are relative to the comparison group in which one finds himself/herself.

For the purposes of this book, the following nine resources are being examined:

FINANCIAL
Having the money to purchase goods and services.

LANGUAGE
Being able to speak and use formal register in writing and in speech.

EMOTIONAL
Being able to choose and control emotional responses, particularly to negative situations, without engaging in self-destructive behavior. This is an internal resource and shows itself through stamina, perseverance, and choices.

MENTAL
Having the mental abilities and acquired skills (reading, writing, computing) to deal with daily life.

SPIRITUAL
Believing in divine purpose and guidance.

PHYSICAL
Having physical health and mobility.

SUPPORT SYSTEMS
Having friends, family, and backup resources available to access in times of need. These are external resources.

RELATIONSHIPS/ROLE MODELS
Having frequent access to adult(s) who are appropriate, who are nurturing to the child, and who do not engage in self-destructive behavior.

KNOWLEDGE OF HIDDEN RULES
Knowing the unspoken cues and habits of a group.

STRATEGY

BEHAVIORAL STRATEGIES	RESEARCHERS	EXPLANATION
Planning for behavior	Agran, M., Blanchard, C., Wehmeyer, M., and Hughes, C. (2001). Coyle, C., and Cole, P. (2004). Feeney, T. J., and Ylvisaker, M. (2008). Feuerstein, R. (1980). Greene, J. A., Moos, D. C., Azevedo, R., and Winters, F. I. (2008). Hamilton, J. L. (2007). King-Sears, M. E. (2008). Kishiyama, M. M., Boyce, W. T., Jimenez, A. M., Perry, L. M., and Knight, R. T. (2008). Mithaug, D. K. (2002). Moore, D. W., Prebble, S., Robertson, J., Waetford, R., and Anderson, A. (2001). Peterson, L. D., Young, K. R., Salzberg, C. L., West, R. P., and Hill, M. (2006).	Planning is related to controlling impulsivity. Also, individuals tend to honor their own plans and not the plans that others make for them.

PLANNING FOR BEHAVIOR

Teaching students to plan teaches impulse control. It is important to note that it's the student who does the planning, not the teacher. As long as the teacher does the planning, the student has not had to do the cognitive work. It's also important to note that, generally, planning is effective only if the plan is written.

PLAN, DO, REVIEW

PLAN FOR THE DAY	STEPS TO DO	REVIEW (HOW DID I DO?)

EXPLANATION

This is another activity sheet that you can use with students to help them with sequencing, planning, following directions, and matching abstract time and tasks. At the beginning of class they answer the question, "What is your plan for today?" They then write the order in which they are going to do the tasks. At the end of class, they answer this question: "Did you do your plan? Why or why not?" For the younger children, the plans can be in the form of drawn pictures. Make photocopies of this form and help students complete the sheet.

STRATEGY

BEHAVIORAL STRATEGIES	RESEARCHERS	EXPLANATION
Building a reward system based on implementing your own plan	Butera, L. M., Giacone, M. V., and Wagner, K. A. (2008). Caine, R. N., and Caine, G. (1991).	Extrinsic rewards work if they are used to start a behavior. Once the behavior is established, extrinsic rewards interfere with the behavior and lessen the behavior. If you tie rewards to the student's ability to complete his/her own plan, then you have established behaviors you want. Once those behaviors are established, then a new plan is made for additional behaviors.

BUILDING A REWARD SYSTEM BASED ON IMPLEMENTING YOUR OWN PLAN

External rewards work as incentives to initiate new behaviors. The research is that if rewards are continued after a behavior is established, then the external reward actually interferes with learning. When you have learners identify rewards based on their own planning, you have started and established an internal reward system that is much more powerful and durable.

STRATEGY

35

BEHAVIORAL STRATEGIES	RESEARCHERS	EXPLANATION
Affirmations	Dweck, C. (2006). Marzano, R., and Arrendondo, D. (1986). Steiner, C. (1994).	Nurturing, positive self-talk allows for task completion, learning new tasks, etc. Very important in learning.

AFFIRMATIONS

Another aspect that affects emotional resources is self-talk, which is simply the internal voice that guides behavior and emotional response. Internal voices are usually developed to some extent from the external environment. Harsh negative parent voices often become internal voices that can be quite damaging. For an in-depth discussion of the effects of internal voices, read the book *Scripts People Live* (2nd Edition) by Claude Steiner (1990).

One of the quickest—and most effective—ways to teach positive self-talk is through daily affirmations. Teachers who use daily affirmations often report increased achievement. Daily affirmations can be written on the board, used in journal writing, and put on the top of homework or tests for extra credit. Positive affirmations provide a supportive internal voice, which acts as a motivator. Below is a list of affirmations that students can use.

1. Every day in every way I am getting better and better.
2. I am responsible for my success.
3. I can win more often when I am educated.
4. I am in control more often when I am educated.
5. I care about _____ and _____ cares about me.
6. I love who I am and who I am becoming.
7. I am respectful of the laws and rules that help us live together in peace.
8. I am grateful for life, now and in the future.
9. I am respectful of every living thing.
10. I am grateful for my studies (work) and I give it my best at all times.
11. I am grateful for my friends and my teachers and my parents.
12. I am grateful that I learn from setbacks and disappointments.
13. I am grateful for the ways in which I am unique and different.
14. If I can do _____, then I can do _____.

STRATEGY

BEHAVIORAL STRATEGIES	RESEARCHERS	EXPLANATION
Service learning	Billig, S. H. (2002). Brooks, R. (1991). Haskitz, A. (1996).	Giving back to the community in service has very high payoffs in developing resilience and adult capacity.

SERVICE LEARNING

Service learning provides the opportunity for students to help each other. Brooks (1991) cites the achievement gains for students who do this.

BEHAVIORAL STRATEGIES	RESEARCHERS	EXPLANATION
Peer mediation	Farrell, A. D., Erwin, E. H., Allison, K. W., Meyer, A., Sullivan, T., Camou, S., et al. (2007). Fisher, R., and Ury, W. (1983). Fisher, R., and Ury, W. (1997). Huan, V. S. (2006). Kunsch, C. A., Jitendra, A. K., and Sood, S. (2007). Schellenberg, R. C., Parks-Savage, A., and Rehfuss, M. (2007). Shamir, A., and Lazerovitz, T. (2007). Shamir, A., Tzuriel, D., and Rozen, M. (2006) Traore, R. (2008). Tzuriel, D., and Shamir, A. (2007).	Teaches questioning and the adult voice; is critical for conflict resolution.

PEER MEDIATION

Peer mediation is critical for conflict resolution. Students are given the language and the adult voice to be able to resolve problems.

STRATEGY

BEHAVIORAL STRATEGIES	RESEARCHERS	EXPLANATION
Storybook to improve behavior	Andreas, S., and Faulkner, C. (1994). Hsu, J. (2008). Seebaum, M. (1999).	Technique developed through drawings and pictures to identify the correct behaviors—especially effective with young children or children with developmental delays.

STORYBOOK TO IMPROVE BEHAVIOR

For young children, using drawings and stories to identify appropriate behaviors is very powerful.

This is a mental model for use with young children to help them identify the appropriate behaviors.

1. Get a blank book.
2. Identify, using stick figures, the student you are working with—e.g., This is you, Robert.
3. Identify his/her feelings when he/she did the behavior—e.g., Robert is mad.
4. Identify what the student actually did—e.g., Robert kicked the teacher.
5. Identify how the victim felt—e.g., Teacher is hurt. Teacher cried.
6. Identify what the student could have said—e.g., I am angry because …
7. Identify what the student's body should do—e.g., Feet should be on the floor.
8. Identify how the student will feel if he/she is doing the behavior correctly—e.g., Robert is calm.
9. Identify how the victim will feel if the student is doing the behavior correctly—e.g., Teacher is calm.

Then have the student read over the pictures until the student can tell the story from the pictures. When the student does the behavior, you present the blank book and tell him/her to read it until he/she can behave appropriately. If the behavior is not in the book, someone (principal, counselor) draws it in the book and makes sure the student can tell it from the pictures before he/she leaves the office.

STRATEGY

39

BEHAVIORAL STRATEGIES	RESEARCHERS	EXPLANATION
Metaphor story	Andreas, S., and Faulkner, C. (1994). Freedman, J., and Combs, G. (1996). Hsu, J. (2008).	Technique from neuro-linguistic programming (NLP) that uses metaphor story to identify causation behind a particular behavior. See Payne (2005) for more information.

USING METAPHOR STORIES

Another technique for working with students and adults is to use a metaphor story. A metaphor story will help an individual voice issues that affect subsequent actions.

A metaphor story does not have any proper names in it and goes like this.

> A student keeps going to the nurse's office two or three times a week. There is nothing wrong with her. Yet she keeps going. Adult says to Jennifer, the girl, "Jennifer, I am going to tell a story and I need you to help me. It's about a fourth-grade girl much like yourself. I need you to help me tell the story because I'm not in fourth grade.
>
> "Once upon a time there was a girl who went to the nurse's office. Why did the girl go to the nurse's office? (Because she thought there was something wrong with her.) So the girl went to the nurse's office because she thought there was something wrong with her. Did the nurse find anything wrong with her? (No, the nurse did not.) So the nurse did not find anything wrong with her, yet the girl kept going to the nurse. Why did the girl keep going to the nurse? (Because she thought there was something wrong with her.) So the girl thought something was wrong with her. Why did the girl think there was something wrong with her? (She saw a TV show ...)"

The story continues until the reason for the behavior is found, and then the story needs to end on a positive note. "So she went to the doctor, and he gave her tests and found that she was OK."

This is an actual case. What came out in the story was that Jennifer had seen a TV show in which a girl her age had died suddenly and had never known she was ill. Jennifer's parents took her to the doctor, he ran tests, and he told her she was fine. So she didn't go to the nurse's office anymore.

A metaphor story is to be used one on one when there is a need to understand the existing behavior and motivate the student to implement the appropriate behavior.

STRATEGY

BEHAVIORAL STRATEGIES	RESEARCHERS	EXPLANATION
Adult voice	Berne, E. (1996). Steiner, C. (1994).	Berne identified three voices that one uses inside the head to direct behavior: child voice, adult voice, and parent voice. Steiner found that if an individual became his/her own parent quite young, or if the primary caregiver was unsympathetic, the individual typically only develops two voices—the child and the negative parent. Without an adult voice, it is very difficult to resolve conflicts or maintain healthy relationships.

ADULT VOICE

The adult voice is used to seek options and ask questions that help resolve a problem. Directly teaching this to students helps them ask their own questions and seek options. It also helps maintain and strengthen relationships.

THREE VOICES

THE CHILD VOICE *
Defensive, victimized, emotional, whining, losing attitude, strongly negative nonverbal.

- Quit picking on me.
- You don't love me.
- You want me to leave.
- Nobody likes (loves) me.
- I hate you.
- You're ugly.
- You make me sick.
- It's your fault.
- Don't blame me.
- She, he, _____ did it.
- You make me mad.
- You made me do it.

* *The child voice is also playful, spontaneous, curious, etc. The phrases listed often occur in conflictual or manipulative situations and impede resolution.*

THE PARENT VOICE * **
Authoritative, directive, judgmental, evaluative, win-lose mentality, demanding, punitive, sometimes threatening.

- You shouldn't (should) do that.

- It's wrong (right) to do _____ .

- That's stupid, immature, out of line, ridiculous.

- Life's not fair. Get busy.

- You are good, bad, worthless, beautiful (any judgmental, evaluative comment).

- You do as I say.

- If you weren't so _____ , this wouldn't happen to you.

- Why can't you be like _____ ?

* *The parent voice can also be very loving and supportive. The phrases listed usually occur during conflict and impede resolution.*

** *The internal parent voice can create shame and guilt.*

THE ADULT VOICE
Nonjudgmental, free of negative nonverbal, factual, often in question format, attitude of win-win.

- In what ways could this be resolved?
- What factors will be used to determine the effectiveness, quality of _____ ?
- I would like to recommend _____ .
- What are choices in this situation?
- I am comfortable (uncomfortable) with _____ .
- Options that could be considered are _____ .
- For me to be comfortable, I need the following things to occur: _____ .
- These are the consequences of that choice/action: _____ .
- We agree to disagree.

Adapted from work of Eric Berne

If you are forced to become your own parent while quite young, you tend to have two of the three voices:

- Child
- Negative parent

The adult voice allows one to resolve a conflict yet still maintain the relationship.

If you have only two voices (child and negative parent), everything is about power and control.

The voice you start in is usually the voice that determines the outcome.

STRATEGY

BEHAVIORAL STRATEGIES	RESEARCHERS	EXPLANATION
Classroom management	Evertson, C. M., and Weinstein, C. S. (2006). Schamberg, M. (2008). Simonsen, B., Fairbanks, S., Briesch, A., Myers, D., and Sugai, G. (2008). Stichter, J. P., Lewis, T. J., Whittaker, T. A., Richter, M., Johnson, N. W., and Trussell, R. P. (2009). Walberg, H. J. (1990). Wong, H. K., and Wong, R. T. (1998).	According to Walberg, up to 65% of achievement can be attributed to classroom management. Ninety-five percent of discipline referrals come the first or last five minutes of class because of lack of procedures.

CLASSROOM MANAGEMENT

Good classroom management allows for more time to be spent on task. It also reduces the "allostatic load" in the brain. Allostatic load is the response of the body's systems to stress (Schamberg, 2008). The more chaotic the environment, the greater the stress. Allostatic load interferes with working memory, which in turn reduces learning.

Procedures Checklist

The following checklist is adapted from Guidelines for the First Days of School, from the Research Development Center for Teacher Education, Research on Classrooms, University of Texas, Austin.

STARTING CLASS	MY PROCEDURE
▪ Taking attendance	
▪ Marking absences	
▪ Tardy students	
▪ Giving makeup work for absentees	
▪ Enrolling new students	
▪ Un-enrolling students	
▪ Students who have to leave school early	
▪ Warm-up activity (that students begin as soon as they walk into classroom)	

INSTRUCTIONAL TIME	MY PROCEDURE
▪ Student movement within classroom	
▪ Use of cellphones and headphones	
▪ Student movement in and out of classroom	
▪ Going to restroom	
▪ Getting students' attention	
▪ Students talking during class	
▪ What students do when their work is completed	
▪ Working together as group(s)	
▪ Handing in papers/homework	
▪ Appropriate headings for papers	

INSTRUCTIONAL TIME	MY PROCEDURE
• Bringing/distributing/using textbooks	
• Leaving room for special class	
• Students who don't have paper and/or pencils	
• Signal(s) for getting student attention	
• Touching other students in classroom	
• Eating food in classroom	
• Laboratory procedures (materials and supplies, safety routines, cleaning up)	
• Students who get sick during class	
• Using pencil sharpener	
• Listing assignments/homework/due dates	
• Systematically monitoring student learning during instruction	

ENDING CLASS	MY PROCEDURE
• Putting things away	
• Dismissing class	
• Collecting papers and assignments	

OTHER	MY PROCEDURE
• Lining up for lunch/recess/special events	
• Walking to lunch/recess	
• Putting away coats and backpacks	
• Cleaning out locker	
• Preparing for fire drills and/or bomb threats	
• Going to gym for assemblies/pep rallies	
• Respecting teacher's desk and storage areas	
• Appropriately handling/using computers/ equipment	

STUDENT ACCOUNTABILITY	MY PROCEDURE
▪ Late work	
▪ Missing work	
▪ Extra credit	
▪ Redoing work and/or retaking tests	
▪ Incomplete work	
▪ Neatness	
▪ Papers with no names	
▪ Using pens, pencils, colored markers	
▪ Using computer-generated products	
▪ Internet access on computers	
▪ Setting and assigning due dates	
▪ Writing on back of paper	
▪ Makeup work and amount of time for makeup work	
▪ Use of cellphones, headphones, iPods, etc., during class	
▪ Letting students know assignments missed during absence	
▪ Percentage of grade for major tests, homework, etc.	
▪ Explaining your grading policy	
▪ Letting new students know your procedures	
▪ Having contact with all students at least once during week	
▪ Exchanging papers	
▪ Using Internet for posting assignments and sending them in	

HOW WILL YOU ...	MY PLAN
• Determine grades on report cards (components and weights of those components)?	
• Grade daily assignments?	
• Record grades so that assignments and dates are included?	
• Have students keep records of their own grades?	
• Make sure your assignments and grading reflect progress against standards?	
• Notify parents when students are not passing or having other academic problems?	
• Contact parents if problem arises regarding student behavior?	
• Contact parents with positive feedback about their child?	
• Keep records and documentation of student behavior?	
• Document adherence to IEP (individualized education plan)?	
• Return graded papers in timely manner?	
• Monitor students who have serious health issues (peanut allergies, diabetes, epilepsy, etc.)?	

BOTH BEHAVIORAL AND ACADEMIC STRATEGIES

STRATEGY

BOTH BEHAVIORAL AND ACADEMIC STRATEGIES	RESEARCHERS	EXPLANATION
Art and music instruction	ART: "The Arts and Educational Reform: Ideas for Schools and Communities." (1994). April, A. (2001). Asbury, C., and Rich, B. (Eds.). (2008). Heath, S. B. (2001). Richards, A. G. (2003). MUSIC: Cox, H. A., and Stephens, L. J. (2006). Gouzouasis, P., Guhn, M., and Kishor, N. (2007). Harris, M. (2008). Kinney, D. W. (2008). Piro, J. M., and Ortiz, C. (2009). Rauscher, F. H. (1999). Southgate, D. E., and Roscigno, V. J. (2009).	Both art and music teach students to translate between an abstract symbol (a note, a drawing) and the sensory sound or object it represents. Music also teaches math.

ART AND MUSIC INSTRUCTION

Art and music instruction teaches students to translate from a concrete reality to an abstract representational (paper/computer) reality. In reading, a symbol (*sh*) represents a sound. Music requires that a student be able to use notes to represent sounds. Music requires math—time is counted and measured in music. This study found that there was a significant difference in the vocabulary and verbal sequencing skills of students who had music instruction compared with those students who did not (see "The Effect of Piano Lessons on the Vocabulary and Verbal Sequencing Skills of Primary Grade Students" by Joseph M. Piro and Camilo Ortiz, *Journal Psychology of Music,* 16 March, 2009).

STRATEGY

43

BOTH BEHAVIORAL AND ACADEMIC STRATEGIES	RESEARCHERS	EXPLANATION
Reframing	Andreas, S., and Faulkner, C. (1994). Chagnon, F. (2007). Elliott, M., Gray, B., and Lewicki, R. (2003). Elliott, M., Kaufman, S., Gardner, R., and Burgess, G. (2002). Fox, J. E. (1999). Jaser, S. S., Fear, J. M., Reeslund, K. L., Champion, J. E., Reising, M. M., and Compas, B. E. (2008). Mills, A. (1999). Nelson, M. (2000). Peters, G. (2002). Rapee, R. M., Gaston, J. E., and Abbott, M. J. (2009). Reddy, L. A., De Thomas, C. A., Newman, E., and Chun, V. (2009). Riley, L. P., LaMontagne, L. L., Hepworth, J. T., and Murphy, B. A. (2007). Scherff, L., and Singer, N. R. (2008).	This NLP technique is one in which the desired behavior is framed against the individual's identity.

REFRAMING

Reframing uses the adult voice to "reframe" the needed behavior in a way that makes sense to the individual and is compatible with his/her own personal identity. For example, rather than see something as a punishment, it becomes an opportunity to learn a new behavior. Rather than seeing physical fighting as a strength, the student is told that it takes more strength to stay out of a fight than to get into one.

STRATEGY

BOTH BEHAVIORAL AND ACADEMIC STRATEGIES	RESEARCHERS	EXPLANATION
Relationships of mutual respect	Comer, J. (1995). Ferguson, R. (2008). Goleman, D. (2006). Greenspan, S. I., and Benderly, B. L. (1997). Payne, R. K. (2005).	No significant learning occurs without a significant relationship. In a research study of 910 first-graders, the at-risk students would not learn from the teacher, even with excellent instructional practices, if they perceived the teacher to be cold and controlling. A significant relationship is one of mutual respect that includes high expectations, insistence, and support.

MUTUAL RESPECT

If a student and teacher do not have a relationship of mutual respect, the learning will be significantly reduced. For some students, learning won't occur at all.

If a student and a teacher don't like each other—or even come to despise each other—forget about significant learning.

If, on the other hand, mutual respect is present, it can compensate for the dislike. Mutual respect is as much about nonverbals as it is about what one says.

Relationships of mutual respect must have three things present:
- Support: the direct teaching of process and mental models
- Insistence: the motivation and persistence that comes from the relationship
- High expectations: the approach of "I know you can do it, and you will"

"No significant learning occurs without a significant relationship."
–Dr. James Comer

STRATEGY

45

BOTH BEHAVIORAL AND ACADEMIC STRATEGIES	RESEARCHERS	EXPLANATION
Planning to control impulsivity	Feuerstein, R. (1980). Schraw, G., Brooks, D., and Crippen, K. J. (2005). Shonkoff, J. P., and Phillips, D. A. (Eds.). (2000).	Feuerstein found that if you cannot plan, you cannot predict. If you cannot predict, you do not know cause and effect. If you do not know cause and effect, you do not know consequence. If you do not know consequence, you do not control impulsivity. If you do not control impulsivity, you have an inclination toward criminal behavior. A neurological study conducted at the University of California, Berkeley, found that poor children's brains have not developed executive functions—one of which is the ability to plan. It can be learned.

PLANNING TO CONTROL IMPULSIVITY

There are several ways to teach impulse control to students. It is important to note that it's the student who does the planning, not the teacher. As long as the teacher does the planning, the student has not had to do the cognitive work. It's also important to note that, generally, planning is effective only if the plan is written.

Planning Backwards. This method of planning has been very successful for many students. Draw a grid with a box for each day the student has before the assignment is due. Label the boxes with the days of the week and dates. Go to the last box—the day the project is due. Below the box make a list of tasks the students must do to finish the assignment. Then ask the students, "What do you have to do the day it is due?" Someone will say, "Hand it in." Then you ask, "What do you have to do the day before it is due?" and often you will get the very first thing that must be done. Eventually, you help the class pace the activities in such a way that the entire project can be done. Then the teacher gives grades two ways: One grade is given regarding the tasks completed each day and the other grade by the final product.

PLANNING BACKWARDS

Monday	Tuesday	Wednesday	Thursday	Friday

EXPLANATION

A technique for helping students deal with time is called planning backwards. You can use this sample sheet to develop your own "planning backwards" activity by starting with the last activity first and moving backwards. For instance, go to the last box—the day the project is due. Below the box have the students make a list of tasks they must do to finish the assignment. Then ask the students, "What do you have to do the day it is due?" Then, "What do you have to do the day before it is due?" and so forth. Eventually you help the class pace the activities in such a way that the entire project can be done.

STRATEGY

BOTH BEHAVIORAL AND ACADEMIC STRATEGIES	RESEARCHERS	EXPLANATION
Relational learning * *This strategy has been repeated because of its significance to working with under-resourced learners. It has applications in this area, as well as where it was first introduced.*	Domagala-Zysk, E. (2006). Faircloth, B. S., and Hamm, J. V. (2005). Good, M., and Adams, G. R. (2008). Green, G., Rhodes, J., Hirsch, A. H., Suarez-Orozco, C., and Camic, P. M. (2008). Guay, F., Marsh, H. W., Senecal, C., and Dowson, M. (2008). Johnson, Lisa S. (2008). Payne, R. K. (2008). Putnam, R. (2000). Reis, S. M., Colbert, R. D., and Hebert, T. P. (2005). Rimm-Kaufman, S. E., and Chiu, Y.-J. I. (2007). Ross, D. D., Bondy, E., Gallingane, C., and Hambacher, E. (2008). Sanchez, B., Reyes, O., and Singh, J. (2006). Scales, P. C., Benson, P. L., Roehlkepartain, E. C., Sesma, A., Jr., and van Dulmen, M. (2006).	Relational learning involves seven characteristics. See Payne (2008).

WHAT IS RELATIONAL LEARNING?

Relational learning involves seven characteristics:

1. Relationships of mutual respect with teachers and administrators
2. A peer group to belong to that is positive and not destructive
3. A coach or advocate who helps the student
4. If not a member of the dominant culture, the student has access to individuals (or histories of individuals) who have attained success and retained connections to their roots
5. Bridging social capital * (e-mail buddies, mentors, et al.) to the larger society
6. At the secondary level, a very specific and clear plan for addressing his/her own learning performance
7. A safe environment (emotionally, verbally, and physically)

* **Social capital** is terminology used by Robert Putnam in his book *Bowling Alone*. It basically means who you know. He identifies two kinds—bonding and bridging. **Bonding** social capital involves people who are like you; **bridging** social capital involves people different from you.

Relational Learning Frame		
Subject Area/Content: Teacher provides structure for academic connectedness	**Social Context:** Teacher provides structure for social connectedness	**Teacher/School as Coach:** Teacher/school provides structure for personal connectedness
■ Content frames ■ Future story ■ Mental models ■ Question making skills ■ Step sheets ■ Study skill sheets ■ Test preparation	■ Classroom atmosphere ■ Classroom interactions ■ Hidden rules ■ Positive peer group ■ Positive physical regard ■ Rapport/respect ■ Registers of language ■ Student interests	■ Connecting future story with school goals ■ Emotional objectivity ■ Evaluating content performance vs. social performance ■ Feedback and praise ■ Generation Y: Who are they? ■ Personal attention ■ Plan for a grade

Developed by Guy Todnem

STRATEGY

47

BOTH BEHAVIORAL AND ACADEMIC STRATEGIES	RESEARCHERS	EXPLANATION
Future story	Adelabu, D. H. (2008). Amyx, D., and Bristow, D. (2004). Bowles, T. (2008). Giota, J. (2006). Greene, B. A., and DeBacker, T. K. (2004). Greene, B. A., Miller, R. B., Crowson, H. M., Duke, B. L., and Akey, K. L. (2004). Horstmanshof, L., and Zimitat, C. (2007). Kaylor, M., and Flores, M. M. (2007). Kerpelman, J. L., Eryigit, S., and Stephens, C. J. (2008). Leondari, A. (2007). Malka, A., and Covington, M. V. (2005). Malmberg, L.-E., Ehrman, J., and Lithen, T. (2005). Phalet, K., Andriessen, I., and Lens, W. (2004). Robbins, R. N., and Bryan, A. (2004). Ryken, A. E. (2006). Seginer, R. (2008). Tabachnick, S. E., Miller, R. B., and Relyea, G. E. (2008).	A future story involves role identity and a future plan that includes education.

FUTURE STORY

A "future story" is a plan for the future. Without it, neither schooling nor work has purpose or significance.

FUTURE STORY   NAME:
You are ten years older than you are now. You are the star of a movie. What are you doing? Who is with you? Circle any of these that are in your future story: children, job, career, marriage/partnership, health, wealth, travel, living in a city, town, rural area, another country, vehicles, hobbies, sports, music, movies, college, technical school, military, church/religion, Internet, video games, friends, family, other.
For which of these reasons do you want to graduate from high school? Keep track of money, I will know I am getting paid correctly, so I can go on to college or military or technical school, to get a better job, to take care of my parents or siblings, to afford my hobbies, to pay for my vehicle, to take care of my children, other.
What do you enjoy doing and would do even if you did not get paid for it? What do you need to do so you can do that AND get paid for doing it?
Who are the friends and adults who will help you get your future story?
WRITE OUT YOUR FUTURE STORY AND INCLUDE HOW EDUCATION WILL HELP YOU GET IT.
Signature: Date:

STRATEGY

48

BOTH BEHAVIORAL AND ACADEMIC STRATEGIES	RESEARCHERS	EXPLANATION
Physical activity	Bailey, R., Armour, K., Kirk, D., Jess, M., Pickup, I., and Sandford, R. (2009). Burton, L. J., VanHeest, J. L. (2007). Chomitz, V. R., Slining, M. M., McGowan, R. J., Mitchell, S. E., Dawson, G. F., and Hacker, K. A. (2009). Ericsson, I. (2008). Ratey, J., and Hageman, E. (2008). Sibley, B. A., Ward, R. M., Yazvac, T. S., Zullig, K., and Potteiger, J. A. (2008). Tomporowski, P. D., Davis, C. L., Miller, P. H., and Naglieri, J. A. (2008). Tremarche, P. V., Robinson, E. M., and Graham, L. B. (2007).	Harvard Research indicates that 45 minutes of exercise at the beginning of the school day significantly raises reading and math scores. The exercise activates brain activity.

PHYSICAL ACTIVITY

Physical activity enhances brain processes. Ratey (2008) provides hard data to confirm that test scores improve when physical activity is done before students engage in academic learning.

STRATEGY

BOTH BEHAVIORAL AND ACADEMIC STRATEGIES	RESEARCHERS	EXPLANATION
Development of role identity	Barnett, R. C., Gareis, K. C., James, J. B., and Steele, J. (2001). Berzonsky, M. D., Branje, S. J. T., and Meeus, W. (2007). Bianchi, A. J., and Lancianese, D. A. (2005). Britsch, B., and Wakefield, W. D. (1998). Burke, P.J., Owens, T.J., Serpe, R., and Thoits, P. A. (Eds.). (2003). Cinamon, R. G., and Rich, Y. (2002). Desrochers, S. (2002). Diemer, M. A. (2002). Gianakos, I. (1995). Kashima, Y., Foddy, M., and Platow, M. (Eds.). (2002). Pasley, K., Furtis, T. G., and Skinner, M. L. (2002). Razumnikova, O. M. (2005).	Role identity is what you want to do or be; it is one of the most effective tools to prevent early pregnancy.

DEVELOPMENT OF ROLE IDENTITY

Role identity is how one sees oneself in a role. For example, "I am a teacher, an administrator, a mother, a father." Those are roles. Many role identities come from work. Success in school and work are linked to role identity.

STRATEGY

50

BOTH BEHAVIORAL AND ACADEMIC STRATEGIES	RESEARCHERS	EXPLANATION
Development of appropriate boundaries	Bagby, J. H., Rudd, L. C., and Woods, M. (2005). Burts, D. C., Schmidt, H. M., Durham, R. S., Charlesworth, R., and Hart, C. H. (2007). Covey, S. (1989). Fraser, M. W., Galinsky, M. J., Smokowski, P. R., Day, S. H., Terzian, M. A., Rose, R. A., et al. (2005). Louv, R. (2006). Petermann, F., and Natzke, H. (2008). Vestal, A., and Jones, N. A. (2004).	Appropriate boundaries are a factor in emotional health. These include boundaries in behavior, relationships, verbal comments, judgments, accusations, physical space, physical touch, bullying, and questions. Must be directly taught.

DEVELOPMENT OF APPROPRIATE BOUNDARIES

Stephen Covey (1989) states that one goes from dependence to independence to interdependence. In the field of addiction, the term co-dependence is used. Boundaries are linked to emotional health, decision making, power, autonomy, and self-governance. As a child, one is dependent—i.e., the adults tell you which behaviors are acceptable, establish boundaries, etc. When the adult is inappropriate (sexual abuse, physical abuse, bullying, using the child to meet the adult's needs), then the child does not learn appropriate behaviors. In adolescence, students tend to be increasingly independent ("I will do what I want to do"). As adults, it's important to be interdependent—i.e., have your own autonomy, yet still be able to work with others. The way this is taught in school tends to be through discipline. For example: Don't have your hands on others, do your own work, etc. Teaching appropriate boundaries is necessary for groups of people, including students, to live together in peace.

STRATEGY

BOTH BEHAVIORAL AND ACADEMIC STRATEGIES	RESEARCHERS	EXPLANATION
Response to Intervention (RTI)	"Assisting Students Struggling with Reading: Response to Intervention and Multi-Tier Intervention in the Primary Grades." (2009). Haager, D., Klingner, J., and Vaughn, S. (Eds.). (2007). McIntosh, K., Campbell, A. L., Carter, D. R., and Dickey, C. R. (2009). Stewart, R. M., Benner, G. J., Martella, R. C., and Marchand-Martella, N. E. (2007).	Response to Intervention is the federally mandated approach for regular education to address special education student needs. This RTI process is embedded as a form of intervention in the six-step process.

RESPONSE TO INTERVENTION (RTI)

RTI (Response to Intervention) is the latest expression of the special education law (Individuals with Disabilities Education Act) and requires that the school make interventions before the student fails. The older version of the IDEA law was a "wait to fail" model. In other words, the student had to fail before he/she received instructional assistance within the regular classroom.

There are three tiers of support. Approximately 80–85% of students fit in the first tier, which is differentiated instruction and relational learning based on the student's resources. The second tier of intervention is focused on the student and the use of staff in an intentionally supportive setting within the regular classroom and curriculum. The third tier of intervention looks specifically at small, structured instructional/behavioral support and is very staff-intensive. All tiers of intervention require progress monitoring.

RTI is not a new program or different curriculum; it is the differentiation of instruction based on measurable goals and timelines that will allow the student to reach grade-level expectations within the regular education curriculum. When the student does not demonstrate sufficient gains based on grade-level expectations, a referral is made to special education for diagnostic assessments of learning.

STRATEGY

52

BOTH BEHAVIORAL AND ACADEMIC STRATEGIES	RESEARCHERS	EXPLANATION
Six-step process	Payne, R. K. (2008).	The six-step process is a simplified procedure developed by Payne that helps buildings address NCLB (No Child Left Behind) and AYP (adequate yearly progress). The steps are outlined in the book *Under-Resourced Learners.* Payne simplified Lezotte's process, creating a relatively easy way to calculate AYP.

SIX-STEP PROCESS

The six-step process involves the following:
1. Gridding students against NCLB chart
2. Aligning time and content grids against the standards
3. Quality instruction
4. Formative assessments
5. Interventions using the RTI process
6. Assigning the activities to the annual school calendar

For more information about this, see Chapter 6 of the *Under-Resourced Learners* book (www.ahaprocess.com).

STRATEGY

BOTH BEHAVIORAL AND ACADEMIC STRATEGIES	RESEARCHERS	EXPLANATION
The R Rules	Souther, E. (2008b).	A semester of scripted lessons to use with at-risk secondary students to teach the knowledge bases, self-assess resource bases, learn the hidden rules, etc. Makes a huge difference in achievement. Can be used as a part of homeroom/advisory time.

THE R RULES

The R Rules is a semester-long workbook written by Elizabeth Souther teaching the hidden rules of school, formal register, self-assessment of resources, etc. It is designed for secondary students and is particularly well suited for at-risk students or alternative education (see www.ahaprocess.com).

**COMMUNITY STRATEGIES
(building human capacity
in adults)**

COMMUNITY STRATEGIES	RESEARCHERS	EXPLANATION
Circles™ Campaign	Miller, S. (2007).	A process of building social bridging capital and support systems for adults in poverty.

CIRCLES™ CAMPAIGN

The Circles™ Campaign is a process by which individuals from poverty build bridging social capital in collaboration with individuals from middle class and/or wealth who become allies in their quest to leave poverty. Money alone does not change thinking. Human capacity development is critical for transition. The intergenerational transfer of knowledge is a key piece of privilege and must be developed as well. The book *Until It's Gone* outlines this model.

STRATEGY

COMMUNITY STRATEGIES	RESEARCHERS	EXPLANATION
Getting Ahead in a Just-Gettin'-By World	Devol, P. E. (2004). Devol, P. E. (2006).	A workbook/program used to develop adult and parent capacity by increasing individual knowledge bases. Individuals in poverty are problem solvers but often don't have the knowledge bases that others have. In a series of 15 lessons people from poverty build knowledge bases. Parents make a future story for themselves and assess their own resource bases.

GETTING AHEAD IN A JUST-GETTIN'-BY WORLD

Getting Ahead in a Just-Gettin'-By World is a workbook for adults in poverty to build their knowledge base. Individuals in poverty are problem solvers but do not necessarily have the same knowledge bases as those from middle class and/or wealth. The *Getting Ahead* workbook is often used in concert with the Circles™ Campaign.

STRATEGY

COMMUNITY STRATEGIES	RESEARCHERS	EXPLANATION
Communities in Schools	Barter, B. (2007). Communities in Schools. (2009). Fain, T., Turner, S., and Ridgeway, G. (2008). Hammond, C., Linton, D., Smink, J., and Drew, S. (2007). Milliken, B. (2007).	Started in 1977, Communities in Schools is an after-school program and support system for students. It can be very effective.

COMMUNITIES IN SCHOOLS

Communities in Schools is an after-school program that builds relationships with students and provides extra assistance. For more insight into this effort, see Bill Milliken's book *The Last Dropout: Stop the Epidemic* (2007).

STRATEGY

COMMUNITY STRATEGIES	RESEARCHERS	EXPLANATION
Collaboration For Kids	Conway, H. W. (2006).	A process developed in Virginia to access all community agencies, judges, law enforcement, etc., to address at-risk behaviors early, with nearly a 90% success rate.

COLLABORATION FOR KIDS

Collaboration For Kids is a model (with a book by the same name) that utilizes community resources to enhance student performance. On the Menominee Indian School District in Keshena, Wisconsin, in the 2007–08 school year, 74 students were positively impacted using the approach. In this approach, red-flag behaviors of students are identified (truancy, medical issues, abuse, etc.), and community agencies work with the schools and parents for successful interventions.

APPENDIXES

Understanding Learning
the How, the Why, the What

Ruby K. Payne, Ph.D.

INTRODUCTION

Teaching vs. Learning

Teaching is outside the head and the body; learning is inside the head and the body.

This book will look at learning—what is inside the head and the body.

Let's make a simplified analogy to a computer. The brain is the hardware; the mind is the software. Learning is about the development and use of the software. Just as hardware and software must have each other in order to function, so the brain must have a mind. So must teaching and learning go together. But they are not the same thing. In order to teach, one must know what needs to go on inside a student's head. That's what this book is.

[For those of you familiar with brain research and cognitive studies, this book is a synopsis of those findings. Please do not be offended by this effort to offer the fruits of that research to a wider audience.]

CHAPTER ONE

The Brain and the Mind

> It is possible to have a brain
> and not have a mind.
> A brain is inherited;
> a mind is developed.
>
> —Feuerstein

To begin our discussion, a distinction will be made between the brain and the mind. Truth be told, it is all one and the same. But for the purposes of this book, the brain is going to mean what you inherited and the mind will be what was developed by your environment. Cognitive scientists have concluded that it's about a 50-50 arrangement. About half of who an individual becomes is developed by his/her genetic code and about half by his/her environment.

All functions of the brain are either a chemical or electrical interaction. A chemical interaction occurs on the face of the cell and continues down the tail (axon) of the cell as an electrical impulse. When the electrical impulse enters the dendrites and synapses, causing their structure to permanently change, learning has occurred.

Therefore, learning is physiological. That's why it takes so long to "unlearn" something that has been learned incorrectly.

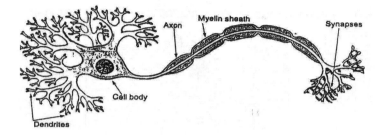

Chemicals in the brain come from four sources: what the genetic code indicates will be made, hormonal fluctuations, external experience (you get frightened and produce adrenaline), and what you eat and breathe.

This book is going to concentrate on the development of the mind. What is the mind as it's being defined here? It's the part that was learned in the environment. But more importantly, it is the abstract replication/representation of external reality. What does that mean?

As human beings, we are very limited. We cannot communicate telepathically. Wouldn't it be nice if we could communicate by, say, rubbing heads? Well, we can't. So we use abstract representational systems, which illustrate common understandings, in order to communicate. Numbers, language, drawings, etc. … all are forms of this.

For example, in the winter, "cold" is measured by a thermometer. However, the sensory reality of cold is not the same as the measured reality of cold. After the temperature gets 10 below zero, it's hard to tell the difference between 10 below zero and 40 below zero. Both are cold. The measurement system is the abstract overlay of the sensory-based reality.

How did we get this abstract structure? We got it from the interplay of language and experience in our environment. When we were young, we were mediated by the adults in our life. What they did when they mediated us was to give us the what, the why, and the how. In other words, they pointed out the stimulus (what we were to pay attention to), gave it meaning (the why), and gave us a strategy (how).

MEDIATION

Point out the stimulus (what)	Give it meaning (why)	Provide a strategy (how)

For example, a parent says to a child:

- "Don't cross the street without looking" (what).
- "You could be killed" (why).
- "Look both ways twice before you cross the street" (how).

This mediation builds an abstract architecture inside the child's head. That architecture acts as an abstract replication of external reality, just as the blueprint acts as an abstract replication of a house.

CHAPTER TWO

Learning (Mediation): How, Why, What

The mediation of the mind happens when an individual is taught the what, the why, and the how. Just as a computer has a programmer for the software, so a student has individuals who help develop the mind. Reuven Feuerstein studied under Jean Piaget and asked him how he accounted for individual differences. Piaget, a biologist, was more interested in accommodation and assimilation. Feuerstein believed that when a caring adult intervened using mediation, significant learning occurred.

Mediation is particularly required when an individual is a new learner to a skill, process, content … whatever.

Research on new learners (Bloom and Berliner) indicates that there is a process that an individual goes through.

NOVICE	Has no experience with information, skill, process, etc. Needs terminology, models, and procedures. Needs context-free rules.
ADVANCED BEGINNER	Has some experience and begins to collect episodic knowledge (stories) and strategic knowledge (strategies). Begins to see similarities across contexts or situations that he/she is in.
COMPETENT	Can make conscious choices about what will and will not work. Can distinguish important from unimportant. Takes personal responsibility for his/her learning because he/she knows what he/she did to make a difference.
PROFICIENT	Sees hundreds of patterns and sorts information quickly by pattern. Uses intuition and know-how to make judgments. Has wealth of experience from which to make generalizations and judgments.
EXPERT	Makes his/her own rules because of extensive experience. Performance is so fluid it can happen virtually without conscious thought; this is called automaticity.

A beginning learner in anything needs the three components of mediation—the what, the why, and the how. Often the expert has difficulty helping a novice because so many of the expert's actions are at the level of automaticity, and the expert has a great deal of difficulty articulating what he/she is doing. This dynamic is frequently seen in sports.

There is a rule in cognitive research that goes like this:

The **more complex the process an individual is involved in, the more parts of that process need to be at the level of automaticity.**

For example, when a child learns to ride a bicycle, training wheels are often used. But a skilled rider would never use training wheels. What the training wheels allow the child to do is learn to steer, guide, pedal, and brake. When those are more at the level of automaticity, then the training wheels are taken off, and additional skills are developed.

So it's a mistake to teach beginners in the same way one would teach a skilled individual.

Second, the brain processes things differently when one is a new learner.

In the book *Making Connections* (1991) by Caine and Caine, the authors describe two different kinds of memory functions in the brain. One is used by beginning learners (taxon), while the other is used by individuals who have more experience with it (locale).

TAXON	LOCALE
No context (experience)	Context (experience)
Memory capacity: about five things	Unlimited memory
Requires continuous rehearsal to remember	Remembers quickly but has loss of accessibility over period of time
Is in short-term memory	Is in long-term memory
Limited to extrinsic motivation	Motivated by novelty, curiosity, expectation (intrinsic)
Specific, habit-like behaviors that are resistant to change	Updated continuously, flexible
Isolated items	Interconnected, spatial memory
Not connected to meaning	Has meaning that is motivated by need to make sense
Acquisition of relatively fixed routes	Forms initial maps quickly and involves sensory activity and emotion; generates personal maps through creation of personal meaning
Follows route	Uses map

What this means is that a beginning learner must be mediated in order to learn. He/she must be given the what, the why, and the how.

Often in schools, the focus is on the content; the why and how are seldom if ever mentioned, so the student is unable to do the work.

CHAPTER THREE

Abstract Representational Systems

One of the reasons you and I are successful is that we have been mediated, not only in sensory data, but also in abstract data. What does that mean?

Just as a computer has icons to represent the software, so does the mind.

A Dutch linguist, Martin Joos, has re-searched language and has found that no matter which language in the world one speaks, there are five registers.

REGISTERS OF LANGUAGE

REGISTER	EXPLANATION
FROZEN	Language that is always the same. For example: Lord's Prayer, wedding vows, etc.
FORMAL	The standard sentence syntax and word choice of work and school. Has complete sentences and specific word choice.
CONSULTATIVE	Formal register when used in conversation. Discourse pattern not quite as direct as formal register.
CASUAL	Language between friends and is characterized by a 400- to 800-word vocabulary. Word choice general and not specific. Conversation dependent upon non-verbal assists. Sentence syntax often incomplete
INTIMATE	Language between lovers or twins. Language of sexual harassment.

The research indicates that there is a strong relationship between the amount of vocabulary an individual has and social class. In generational poverty, it is not unusual for individuals to know only casual register. An individual who has only casual register does not have many abstract words. The abstract words are in formal register.

Hart and Risley in *Meaningful Differences in the Everyday Experience of Young American Children* (1995) found the following patterns in children between the ages of 1 and 4 in stable households.

Economic group	Number of words exposed to
Welfare households	13 million words
Working-class households	26 million words
Professional households	45 million words

Language or words are the tools of ideas. Abstract words represent those ideas, concepts, processes, etc., that do not have sensory-based representations.

WHAT ARE THESE ABSTRACTIONS OR REPRESENTATIONS?

A few summers ago it was so hot in Fort Worth, Texas, that the railroad tracks warped. We keep butter out in our house, and it kept melting. One day I said to my husband, "The thermometer says it's 72 degrees in here, but the butter is melting. In the winter, it says 72 degrees and the butter does not melt." He said, "Do not confuse real heat with measured heat."

You see, Anders Celsius and Gabriel Fahrenheit decided they wanted a better way to talk about heat, so each designed a system to do so. But the systems are abstract representations and measurements of a sensory-based reality.

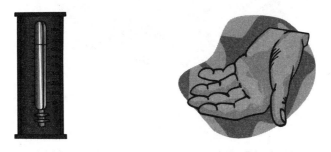

Language is the tool we use to create and acknowledge those abstract systems. Abstract systems are learned. If a student comes from an environment where there is a heavy reliance on casual register, and there isn't much formal education, often the student has few abstract representational systems. **To survive in poverty, one must be very sensory-based and non-verbal. To survive in school, one must be very verbal and abstract.**

Furthermore, abstractions are stored in the mind in either visual or auditory rhythmic memory. Abstractions are kept in mental models. **Mental models are in the form of a story, a metaphor, an analogy—or, perhaps, a two-dimensional drawing.**

For example, when a house is being built, blueprints are used. The blueprints become the abstract representational system for the final sensory-based object, the house.

Another example: A lawyer I know got a call from a colleague who was in court and needed a piece of paper from his desk. She said, "Your desk is a mess. No one could find it." And he said to her, "Go stand in front of my desk. Picture an overlay of the map of the United States. That paper is somewhere around Vermont." And she found it. He had given her an abstract representational system.

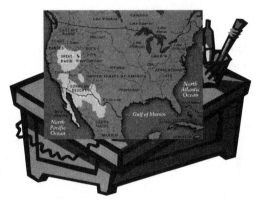

Mental models tell either the purpose, structure, or pattern of a subject area or discipline.

To survive in the world of work or school, one must be able to use abstract representational systems. They are learned.

CHAPTER FOUR

Abstract Processes
(the How)

Abstract processes are "the how" and accompany all learning. Jerome Bruner says all learning is connected to the task and context of the learning. In other words, the process and the content are interwoven. To teach one without the other is to have incomplete learning.

Just as one must follow steps in software, i.e., double-click the icon, then do this ... so the mind must have procedures.

Often in schools, we do not direct-teach the process. We direct-teach the content. Reuven Feuerstein describes the abstract processes that must be used to learn.

INPUT STRATEGIES

Input is defined as "quantity and quality of the data gathered."
1. Use planning behaviors.
2. Focus perception on specific stimulus.
3. Control impulsivity.
4. Explore data systematically.
5. Use appropriate and accurate labels.
6. Organize space with stable systems of reference.
7. Orient data in time.
8. Identify constancies across variations.
9. Gather precise and accurate data.
10. Consider two sources of information at once.
11. Organize data (parts of a whole).
12. Visually transport data.

ELABORATION STRATEGIES

Elaboration is defined as "use of the data."
1. Identify and define the problem.
2. Select relevant cues.
3. Compare data.
4. Select appropriate categories of time.
5. Summarize data.
6. Project relationships of data.
7. Use logical data.
8. Test hypotheses.
9. Build inferences.
10. Make a plan using the data.
11. Use appropriate labels.
12. Use data systematically.

OUTPUT STRATEGIES

Output is defined as "communication of the data."
1. Communicate clearly the labels and process.
2. Visually transport data correctly.
3. Use precise and accurate language.
4. Control impulsive behavior.

Where does an individual get these strategies? Mediation builds them! Typically in school we start teaching at the elaboration level, i.e., the use of the data. When students don't understand, we reteach these strategies but don't revisit the quality and quantity of the data gathered—namely, the input strategies.

In order to better understand input strategies, each is explained in more detail. Typically, input strategies are not directly taught, because we don't know how to teach them. The assumption is that everyone has them. For those students who don't have these strategies, however, the strategies can be directly taught to students.

INPUT STRATEGIES

Using planning behaviors includes goal setting, identifying the procedures in the task, identifying parts of the task, assigning time to the task(s), and identifying the quality of the work necessary to complete the task.

Focusing perception on a specific stimulus is the strategy of seeing every detail on the page or in the environment. It is the strategy of identifying everything noticed by the five senses.

Controlling impulsivity is the strategy of stopping action until one has thought about the task. There is a direct correlation between planning and impulse control.

Exploring data systematically means that a strategy is employed to procedurally and systematically go through every piece of data. Numbering is a way to go systematically through data. Highlighting important data is another way.

Using appropriate and accurate labels (vocabulary) is the precise use of words to identify and explain. If a student does not have specific words to use, then his/her ability to retrieve and use information is severely limited. It's not enough that a student can do a task, he/she also must be able to label the procedures, tasks, and processes so that the task can be successfully repeated each time and analyzed at a metacognitive level. Metacognition is the ability to think about one's thinking. To do so, labels must be attached. Only when labels are attached can the task be evaluated and, therefore, improved.

Organizing space with stable systems of reference is crucial to success in math. It means that up, down, across, right, left, horizontal, vertical, diagonal, east, west, north, south, etc., are understood. It means that an individual can identify with words the position of an item. It means an individual can organize space. For example, he/she can find things on a desk. It means that a person can read a map. If an individual does not have this ability, then it's virtually impossible to tell a *p* from a *b* from a *d*. The only differentiation is the orientation to space.

Orienting data in time is the strategy of assigning abstract values to time and the use of the measurements of time. Without an abstract sense of time that includes a past, present, and future, a student cannot plan, he/she cannot sequence, and he/she cannot match time and task (and, therefore, doesn't get work done).

Identifying constancies across variations is the strategy of knowing what always remains the same and what changes. For example, if you don't know what always makes a square a square, you cannot identify constancies. This strategy enables the individual to define things, to recognize a person or an object, and to compare and contrast. This strategy also allows cursive writing to be read in all its variations.

Gathering precise and accurate data is the use of specific vocabulary and word choice, identifying precisely when something occurred in time and where it occurred in space, knowing the constancies, and exploring the data systematically.

Considering two sources of information at once means that the mind can hold two objects simultaneously and compare and contrast the two objects. To do this, the individual must be able to visually transport data accurately, identify the constancies and variations, and go through the data systematically. When those processes are completed, the student must be able to assign new vocabulary (if things have changed) and reassign existing vocabulary.

Organizing data (parts of a whole) involves going through data systematically, organizing space, identifying constancies and variations, and using vocabulary to label both the parts and the whole.

Visually transporting data is when the eye picks up data, then carries it accurately into the brain, examines it for constancies and variations, and labels the parts and the whole. If a student cannot visually transport data, then he/she often cannot read, has difficulty with basic identification of anything, and cannot copy.

WHAT DOES THIS MEAN IN THE CLASSROOM?

When a student cannot:	One will often see this:
Use planning behaviors …	Does not get his/her work done, is impulsive.
Focus perception on a specific stimulus …	Misses parts of the task; cannot find the information on the page.
Control impulsivity …	Cannot plan.
Explore data systematically …	Does not have a method for checking work, for getting all the work done, and for finding complete answers.
Use appropriate and accurate labels (vocabulary) …	Does not have the words to explain; cannot label processes; uses generic words, e.g., "Get that thing."
Organize space with stable systems of reference …	Cannot read a map; cannot use the procedures in math
Orient data in time …	Cannot sequence or plan; cannot follow directions.
Identify constancies across variations …	Cannot make judgments or generalizations; cannot identify patterns.
Gather precise and accurate data …	Cannot tell specifically when, where, and how something happened.
Consider two sources of information at once …	Cannot compare and contrast; does a different assignment the way the first one was done, whether appropriate or not.
Organize data (parts of a whole) …	Cannot explain why; does not recognize when something is missing.
Visually transport data …	Cannot cheat because he/she cannot copy.

HOW DOES THE TEACHER EMBED THESE PROCESSES AND DEVELOP MINDS?

One way is to teach these processes with all content to all students. The way I approached it in my teaching career was to use four simple processes—sorting, question making, planning to control impulsivity, and planning and labeling tasks—because these processes embed into all content, use all the input strategies, and are quick and easy.

1 Sorting, Using Patterns

In brain research what is fairly clear is that the information must be sorted or "chunked" in order to be remembered. Details are not remembered over time, but patterns are. So if you teach patterns directly and then teach students to sort what is and is not important in relation to the patterns, the students will learn much more quickly.

In problem solving at work or school, it's very important that the worker or student is able to sort through a great deal of information quickly. He/she does this by going through patterns. For example, if you want to buy shoes at a department store, you don't wander aimlessly through the store. You know that a department store is arranged in predictable patterns. You find the shoe department.

So for any content you're teaching, teach the patterns and mental models of the content. That will help students sort what is and is not important in the learning.

2 Question Making

A quick approach is to give students the question stems and then have them use the rules to develop a multiple-choice question. Developing multiple-choice questions develops critical-thinking skills. Some examples follow.

READING-OBJECTIVE QUESTION STEMS

Objective 1: Word Meaning

In this story the word _____ means …

The word _____ in this passage means …

Objective 2: Supporting Ideas

What did _____ do after …?

What happened just before _____ …?

What did _____ do first? Last?

According to the directions given, what was _____ supposed to do first?

After _____? Last?

Where does this story take place?

When does the story take place?

Objective 3: Summarizing Written Texts

Which sentence tells the main idea of the story?

This story is mainly about …

What is the main idea of paragraph 3?

What is the story mostly about?

Which statement best summarizes this passage (paragraph)?

Objective 4: Perceiving Relationships and Recognizing Outcomes

Why did __ (name) __ do __ (action) ___?

What will happen as a result of _____?

Based on the information, which is _____ most likely to do?

What will happen to _____ in this story?

You can tell from this passage that _____ is most likely to …

Objective 5: Analyzing Information to Make Inferences and Generalizations

How did _____ feel about _____?

How does _____ feel at the beginning (end) of the story?

According to Figure 1, what … (or where … how many … when …) is …?

The ___ (event) ___ is being held in order to …

By ___ (action) ___, ___ (name) ___ was able to show that …

You can tell from this passage that …?

Which word best describes _____'s feelings in this passage?

Objective 6: Distinguishing Between Fact and Opinion

Which of these is a fact expressed in the passage?

Which of these is an opinion expressed in the passage?

QUESTION-MAKING STEMS
(from Texas Assessment of Academic Skills)

1. What does the word _____ mean?
2. What can you tell from the following passage?
3. What does the author give you reason to believe?
4. What is the best summary of this passage?
5. Which of the following is a **fact** in this passage?
6. What is the main idea of the _____ paragraph?
7. Which of the following is an opinion in this passage?
8. What happens after _____?
9. How did _____ feel when _____?
10. What is the main idea of this passage?
11. Which of these happened (first/last) in the passage?
12. Which of these is **not** a fact in the passage?
13. Where was _____?
14. When did _____?
15. What happens when _____?
16. What was the main reason for the following _____?
17. After _____, what could _____?
18. Where does the _____ take place?
19. Which of these best describes _____ before/after _____?

Taken from Julie Ford

MORE QUESTION-MAKING STEMS

1. From this passage (story), how might _____ be described?
2. Why was _____?
3. Why did _____?
4. How else might the author have ended the passage (story)?
5. If the author had been _____, how might the information have been different?
6. In this passage, what does _____ mean?
7. How did _____ feel about _____?
8. What caused _____ to _____?
9. What is _____?
10. When _____ happened, why did _____?
11. The passage states that _____.
12. Why is that information important to he reader?

3 Planning to Control Impulsivity

Planning is the key to the tasks that get finished and to the control of impulsivity. Even more importantly, brain research indicates that the primary filter for what gets noticed by the mind is closely correlated with the goals of the person. So when there is no planning, there are no goals. Emotional need or association, then, determines activities.

To teach planning it's important to teach students to plan backwards. Stephen Covey, in *The Seven Habits of Highly Successful People* (1989), says, "Begin with the end in mind." In order to accomplish this "backwards planning," the teacher simply has students go to the end first, then the day or task before that, and so forth.

It's also very important in the planning process that abstract time (minutes, hours, days, weeks) gets assigned to the task.

PLANNING BACKWARDS

Monday	Tuesday	Wednesday	Thursday	Friday

4 Planning and Labeling Tasks

In addition to controlling impulsivity, planning allows a person to finish tasks. To complete tasks, both labels (vocabulary) and procedures must be used. In addition, teachers need a method for addressing each part of the task, i.e., having a systematic method for getting it all done and checking to see that it has been done.

Process (the how) is crucial to any learning; this must be taught.

In the following example, a battery is made. The left-hand column (on page 217) tells the steps that were followed. The right-hand column tells **why.** In the left-hand column ...

Step 1 The student fills a bowl with vinegar.
Step 2 The student puts pieces of cloth in the vinegar and squeezes them out.
Step 3 The student takes a piece of copper and a piece of zinc and puts the squeezed-out cloth between the copper and zinc.
Step 4 The student makes four of the items identified in Step 3.
Step 5 A piece of aluminum foil is put on the bottom of the stack of four and curved to the top of the stack.
Step 6 A small light connects the foil pieces and the stack of four. If the light goes on, the battery is completed.

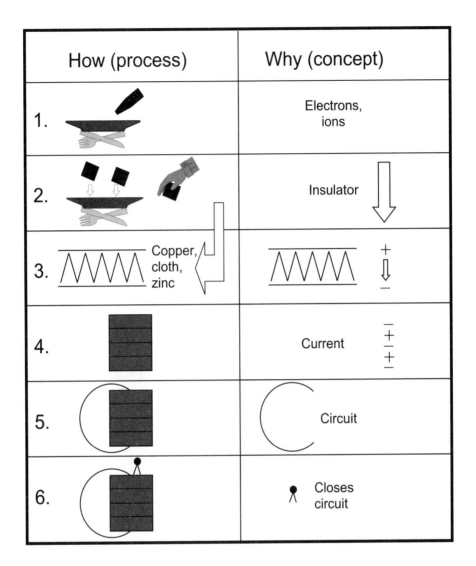

How (process)	Why (concept)
1.	Electrons, ions
2.	Insulator
3. Copper, cloth, zinc	+ –
4.	Current + – +
5.	Circuit
6.	Closes circuit

On the right-hand side is the label, or the why …

Step 1   Why do we need the vinegar? *Because it provides electrons and ions.*
Step 2   Why do we need the cloth dipped in vinegar? *Because it provides a conductor and insulator.*
Step 3   Why do we need the copper and zinc? *Because they give and take electrons.*
Step 4   Why do we need the stack of four? *Because it makes a current.*
Step 5   Why do we need the aluminum foil? *Because it makes a circuit.*
Step 6   Why do we need the light? *To close the circuit.*

CHAPTER FIVE

Mental Models Blueprints of the Subject Matter
(the Why)

1 Mental models are how the mind holds abstract information, i.e., information that has no sensory representation.

Each of us carries much abstract information around in our head every day. How do we do this? We carry it in mental models.

Just as a computer has a file manager to represent the structure of the software content, so does the human mind.

2 All subject areas or disciplines have their own blueprints or mental models.

In other words, they have their own way to structure information. For two people to communicate, there must be shared understanding.

This shared understanding comes from the study of subject matter. All occupations and all disciplines have their own mental models. To communicate about that occupation or discipline, an understanding of those mental models (abstract blueprints) is necessary.

3 Mental models tell us what is and is not important in the discipline. They help the mind sort.

4 **Mental models often explain "the why" of things working the way they do.**

5 **Mental models tell the structure, purpose, or pattern.**

That's how the mind sorts what is and is not important. The mind can only remember when it can "chunk" and sort information.

6 **Mental models are held in the mind as stories, analogies, or two-dimensional drawings.**

7 **Mental models "collapse" the amount of time it takes to teach something.**

8 **Mental models of a discipline are contained within the structure of the curriculum.**

To illustrate, math is about assigning order and value to the universe. We tend to assign order and value in one of three ways: numbers, space, or time. Fractions, for example, are a part of math curricula because fractions are the shared understanding of parts to whole of *space*. Decimals are studied because decimals tell parts to whole of *numbers*.

Lee Shulman found in his research that the difference between a good and excellent teacher is the depth of understanding the latter has of the discipline.

What are examples of mental models? Teachers have used them forever. But, too often, educators haven't found ways to share them with other teachers. They are the drawings, the verbal stories, the analogies that are given as part of instruction. As one teacher said, "It is how I explain it."

For example, in math a square number is a square number because it physically forms a square. Nine is a square number.

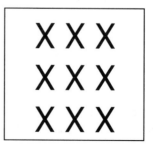

When the root of a square number is discussed, it's very easy to understand. The square root of 9 is 3 because no matter how you draw the lines you will always get 3. In 30 seconds you, the reader, now understand the concept of a square number and a square root.

A mental model to help understand the pattern in the multiplication of positive and negative numbers is found in this short pictorial story.

MULTIPLYING POSITIVE AND NEGATIVE NUMBERS

+ Good guy - Bad guy	+ Coming to town - Leaving town	Get
+ + - -	+ - + -	+ - - +

So, for example, the good guys (+) are coming to town (+), which is good. Translated to math, it would read: a positive number (+) multiplied by a positive number (+) yields a positive number (+), and so on.

9 There are generic mental models.

In addition to having mental models for subject areas or disciplines, there also are mental models for occupations. To be successful in work or school one must have four generic mental models. They are: space, time, part to whole, and formal register. These mental models are basic to all tasks.

SPACE

Space becomes important because your body operates in space. The mind must have a way to keep track of your body. One way is to touch everything. Another way is to assign a reference system to space using abstract words and drawings. For example, we talk about east, west, north, south, up, down, etc. Because math is about assigning order and value to the universe, we tend to do it directionally. Another illustration: We write small to large numbers from left to right. To read a map, one must have a reference for space. To find things in your office or desk, there must be an abstract referencing system for space.

One way to initially teach the concept of space is as follows ...

On which side of the tip of the arrow is the dot?

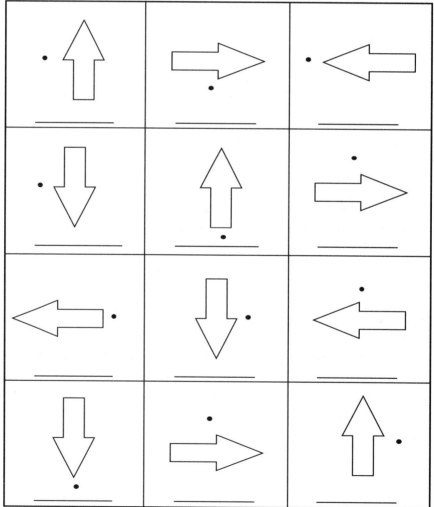

TIME

A mental model for abstract time (days, minutes, weeks, hours, etc.) is crucial to success in school and work. One way to keep time is emotionally (how it feels), but another is abstractly with a calendar or a clock. Past, present, and future must be in the mental model because, without these, it isn't possible to sequence.

If you cannot sequence, then …	You cannot plan.
If you cannot plan, then …	You cannot predict.
If you cannot predict, then …	You cannot identify cause and effect.
If you cannot identify cause and effect, then …	You cannot identify consequence.
If you cannot identify consequence, then …	You cannot control impulsivity.
If you cannot control impulsivity, then …	You have an inclination toward criminal behavior.

PART TO WHOLE

Part to whole means that one can identify the parts, as well as the whole. For example, chapters make a book. Words make a sentence. You cannot analyze anything unless you understand part to whole.

FORMAL REGISTER

Because formal register is the language currency of work and school, it becomes crucial to have an understanding of it. Simple tools have been developed for Project Read® by Language Circle Enterprises, Inc. Some Project Read examples would look like this.

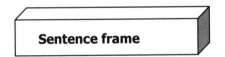

Sentence frame

Reminds me that a sentence must have a capital letter at the beginning and a stop sign at the end. ⸱ The effect of the sentence is expressed by the question mark (?) above the period or the exclamation point (!) above the period.

? . !

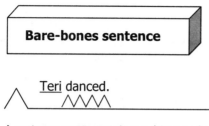

Bare-bones sentence

Teri danced.

A sentence must contain a subject and a predicate. The predicate can be an action predicate word.

The subject names a person, place, thing, or idea.

The action of the subject expresses physical or mental action, such as the following examples.

moved   kicked   thought   imagined

Or the predicate can be a bound predicate.

Teri is dancing.

Predicate expanders

The predicate can be expanded by expressing the

how   when   where   why   of the action.

Example:

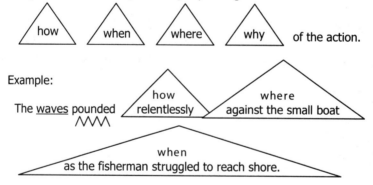

The waves pounded   how relentlessly   where against the small boat

when as the fisherman struggled to reach shore.

Predicate expanders:

How   = degree   adverbs (-ly ending, like or as, with/without)
When   = time   before, during, after, when, while, since
Where   = position   prepositional phrases (to, from, against,
                         behind)
Why   = reason   because, to, so, for

(The opening sentence of each new paragraph should contain four expanders.)

Subject describers

Words that describe physical characteristics, personality, numbers, and ownership.

Source: Project Read® excerpt reprinted with permission of copyright holder, Language Circle Enterprises, Inc., and their creators Victoria Greene and Mary Lee Enfield, Ph.D. Contact: (800) 450-0343. www.projectread.com

10 Sketching is a technique that can be used in the classroom to identify each student's mental models.

Simply ask students to sketch (draw in two dimensions) what a word or concept means to them. If they cannot sketch anything, it probably is not inside their head.

EXAMPLES OF SKETCHING:

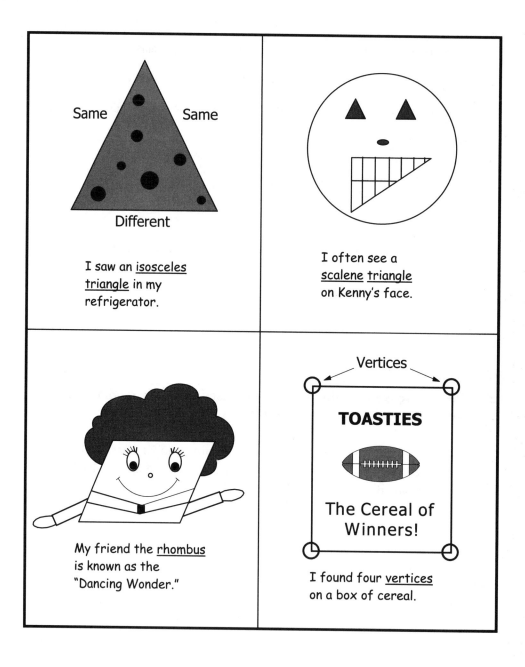

Same   Same

Different

I saw an <u>isosceles</u>
<u>triangle</u> in my
refrigerator.

I often see a
<u>scalene</u> <u>triangle</u>
on Kenny's face.

My friend the <u>rhombus</u>
is known as the
"Dancing Wonder."

Vertices

TOASTIES

The Cereal of
Winners!

I found four <u>vertices</u>
on a box of cereal.

Using mental models makes both teaching *and* learning much easier.

CHAPTER SIX

Content
(the What)

The content—or "the what" of learn-ing—is the part of instruction that is usually focused on. When the processes (the how) and the blueprints of the sub-ject matter (the why) are direct-taught, the content tends to fall into place.

Just as a computer has files, so does the mind.

Content is organized by the constructs of the disciplines (or the mental models). Here are some examples.

Content	Purpose
Language Arts	Using structure and language to communicate
Math	Assigning order and value to the universe
Biology	Identifying living systems and relationships within and among those systems
Chemistry	Bonding
Algebra	Solving for the unknown through functions
Geometry	Using logic to order and assign values to form and space
Physics	Using matter and energy through math applications
Social Studies	Identifying patterns of people and governments over time
Earth Science	Identifying and predicting physical phenomena

For example, because Language Arts is about using structure and language to communicate, virtually all Language Arts curriculum at the secondary level is divided by genres, i.e., poetry, drama, grammar, etc. Those curriculum divisions end up reflecting the structures of the various disciplines.

WHY IS THIS IMPORTANT?

The structure of the discipline becomes significant because it identifies what is and is not important. The research indicates that instructional time is a huge factor in learning.

So the questions in this context are: Is it cute or does it count? Does the information presented/explored promote an understanding of the constructs and use of the discipline?

When teachers or other staff persons in a building are deciding "the what" of learning (namely, the content), it's very important to address the amount of time that will be given to learning that chunk of information.

WHY IS THIS IMPORTANT TO THE LEARNER?

If adequate time is not spent on what is important—on what counts—the learner will not have learned enough to sort what is and isn't important in that subject area. Therefore, the learner will not be able to use the information in any competent manner.

CHAPTER SEVEN

Motivation for Learning

Probably the most frequently asked question by teachers is this: How can I get my students to want to learn? Dr. James Comer says it best:

> No significant learning
> occurs without a significant
> relationship
> [of mutual respect].
>
> —Comer

What does that mean? Quite simply (going back to the computer analogy), if there isn't someone at the keyboard or entering via voice, nothing happens.

And so it is with learning. It requires human interaction. At the heart of all learning are relationships.

HOW DO YOU RECOGNIZE RELATIONSHIPS OF MUTUAL RESPECT?

Generally, in relationships of mutual respect, three things are present:

Support, insistence, and high expectations

How do support, insistence, and high expectations show up in the classroom? Support becomes the direct-teaching of process and mental models; insistence is the motivation and persistence that comes from the relationship; and high expectations constitute the approach of "I know you can do it, and you will."

When there isn't mutual respect, one person becomes the taker, and the other becomes the giver. Eventually both parties come to dislike or even despise each other.

Many teachers believe that if they are nice to students, students will be nice to them. Not so. Mutual respect is taught, and mutual respect is learned.

ALL LEARNING IS DOUBLE-CODED

In the book *The Growth of the Mind and the Endangered Origins of Intelligence* (1997), Stanley Greenspan and Beryl Benderly say all learning is double-coded, both mentally and emotionally.

It's very important to understand the emotional underpinnings of learning. All learning is in essence emotional, and virtually all learning starts with significant relationships.

The primary motivator for the development of each stage is a significant relationship.

Six developmental stages in the learning process occur when relationships are supportive and nurturing.

These six stages are:

STAGE	EXPLANATION
1. Ability to attend	To pay attention to the sensory data in the environment. The earliest sensory data—touch, taste, sound, smell, sight—result from the interplay of relationships.
2. Ability to engage	To experience feelings—joy, pleasure, anger, emotional warmth, disappointment, assertiveness, etc. Intimacy and relating begin at this stage.
3. Ability to be intentional	To create and direct desire. To use non-verbals with purpose and intention. For example, I (as an infant) want you to hold me, so I hold up my arms, and you pick me up.
4. Ability to form complex interactive patterns	To connect and use one's own intentional signals in interaction with another to negotiate and to receive security, acceptance, and approval.
5. Ability to create images, symbols, and ideas	To give abstract mental constructs emotional meaning and significance. This is the basis of reasoning and emotion-based coping strategies. When images, symbols, and ideas don't have emotional investment, they are fragmented.
6. Ability to connect images, symbols, and ideas	To develop the infrastructure and architecture of the mind. To "image" one's own feelings and desires and to understand emotional signals from others.

In discussing the six stages, one overriding reality must be remembered:

Emotion organizes experience and behavior.

STAGE ONE: ABILITY TO ATTEND

At the very beginning of learning, the infant must sort out what the sensations are and what they mean. Those earliest sensations almost always come through relationships. Someone is holding the child. Someone is feeding the child. The child must stay calm enough to notice the sensations he/she is experiencing. The child must find patterns in the sensations. From these patterns come security and order. From this security and order comes the ability to regulate the mind.

STAGE TWO: ABILITY TO ENGAGE

When young children can attend to the surroundings and actions of the people who are their caretakers, they become engaged. The caretaker smiles, and they smile. In short, the child mirrors the expressions of the caretaker.

Greenspan and Benderly say it well:

> Without some degree of this ecstatic wooing by at least one adult who adores her, a child may never know the powerful intoxication of human closeness, never abandon herself to the magnetic pull of human relationships … Whether because her nervous system is unable to sustain the sensations of early love or her caregiver is unable to convey them, such a child is at risk of becoming self-absorbed or an unfeeling, self-centered, aggressive individual who can inflict injury without qualm or remorse (p. 51).

STAGE THREE: ABILITY TO BE INTENTIONAL

At this preverbal stage, a purposeful exchange of signals and responses is used to elicit what the child desires. In this stage the child learns to distinguish between you and me, i.e., from self and other. Boundaries are established. When responses are inappropriate, the child becomes disorganized and eventually loses interest. For example, if a person is talking to someone with a "poker face," eventually the conversation becomes fragmented; the speaker loses interest and gives up.

Interactions become purposeful, and "willful reciprocity" occurs, which also signals a higher developmental level of the central nervous system.

Desires or wishes are tied to actions, not ideas. Desires or wishes also are linked to subjective needs, not objective needs.

STAGE FOUR: ABILITY TO FORM COMPLEX INTERACTIVE PATTERNS

At this stage, purpose and interaction become the focus. The child learns to communicate across space, i.e., I am not touching my caregiver. She is in the next room, but I know she is there. This gives a strong sense of emotional security. Imitation is a part of this stage. The child mimics what the adult does. At this stage, a child's emotions are attached to patterns of response. Attitudes and values start here. Meaning is established from patterns of desire, expectation, and intention.

STAGE FIVE: ABILITY TO CREATE IMAGES, SYMBOLS, AND IDEAS

Here the child experiences himself/herself in images—and not just in feelings, physical sensations, and behavior. It's important to note that children who haven't mastered the previous stages tend to operate in a concrete, rote manner. At this point in time, individuals can try out behaviors and actions inside their head without actually doing them.

STAGE SIX: ABILITY TO CONNECT IMAGES, SYMBOLS, AND IDEAS

At this stage, the individual connects the images, symbols, and ideas that were developed in Stage Five to an architecture in which abstractions are emotionally embedded and interwoven. The individual is able to view emotions abstractly and work through them both at a feeling level and a cognitive one. Sorting occurs both cognitively and through emotion.

LEARNING THE ABSTRACT

Because schools and the work setting operate at stages five and six, many individuals are new learners to the abstract. There is a process that a person goes through when he/she is learning something new. That process was discussed in Chapter Two.

HOW DOES A STUDENT KNOW THAT A TEACHER HAS RESPECT FOR HIM/HER?

Two pieces of research are particularly instructive. One is from Stephen Covey, and the other is research by TESA (Teacher Expectations and Student Achievement).

Covey states that relationships of mutual respect are like bank accounts. You make emotional deposits to those relationships, and you make emotional withdrawals from the relationships. When the withdrawals are substantially greater than the deposits, the relationship is soon broken.

DEPOSITS	WITHDRAWALS
Seek first to understand	Seek first to be understood
Keeping promises	Breaking promises
Kindnesses, courtesies	Unkindnesses, discourtesies
Clarifying expectations	Violating expectations
Loyalty to the absent	Disloyalty, duplicity
Apologies	Pride, conceit, arrogance
Open to feedback	Rejecting feedback

Chart adapted from *The 7 Habits of Highly Effective People* (1989) by Stephen Covey

The TESA research describes 15 behaviors that teachers use with students when there is mutual respect between teacher and student. The study found that when these behaviors are used with all students, learning jumps dramatically.

Here are the 15 behaviors of mutual respect:

1. Calls on everyone in the room equitably.
2. Provides individual help.
3. Gives "wait time" (allows student enough time to answer).
4. Asks questions to give the student clues about the answer.
5. Asks questions that require more thought.
6. Tells students whether their answers are right or wrong.
7. Gives specific praise.
8. Gives reasons for praise.
9. Listens.
10. Accepts the feelings of the student.
11. Gets within an arm's reach of each student each day.
12. Is courteous to students.
13. Shows personal interest and gives compliments.
14. Touches students (appropriately).
15. Desists (does not call attention to every misbehavior).

TESA copyright is held by Los Angeles Board of Education.

When we asked students in our research how they knew the teacher had respect for them, repeatedly we heard the following:

- The teacher calls me by my name, not "Hey you."
- The teacher answers my questions.
- The teacher cares about me.
- The teacher talks to me respectfully.
- The teacher notices me and says hi.
- The teacher helps me when I need help.

WHAT DOES THIS MEAN IN PRACTICE?

1 If a student and teacher don't have a relationship of mutual respect, the learning will be significantly reduced and, for some students, it won't occur at all.

2 If a student and teacher don't like each other—or even come to despise each other—forget about significant positive learning. If mutual respect is present, that can compensate for the dislike.

CHAPTER EIGHT

Difficult Students, Difficult Classrooms

THESE QUESTIONS INEVITABLY COME UP:

What do I do when more than 40% of the students are difficult? How can learning take place with so many difficult students?

What do I do with a student who habitually breaks relationships with adults?

What do I do with the student who has biochemical issues? Has neurological damage?

To use our analogy to the computer, what do I do when the computer freezes? When the hard drive crashes? When the software doesn't do what it's supposed to?

As you know, just like the computer, not everything can be "fixed." But what we do know are ways to minimize the interruptions and address the learning.

SOME SUGGESTIONS:

1. **Always direct-teach the mental models of the content you are teaching.** Fewer discipline problems occur when students are learning.

2. **Direct-teach the processes and procedures you want to occur in your classroom.** Have students practice those. Remember that 95% of discipline problems in classrooms occur the first five and last five minutes of class. Harry Wong, in his book *The First Day of School* (1998), has a number of excellent suggestions.

3. **Build relationships of mutual respect with the "troublemakers."** Ninety percent of discipline problems come from 10% of the students. Humor (not sarcasm) is one of the best tools for developing mutual respect; students particularly look to see if you have a sense of humor about yourself. Furthermore, students won't respect you unless you are personally strong. So if you show fear, you won't be respected.

4. **Tightly structure tasks by time and procedure.** Do so by giving students the steps—in writing—necessary to do the task, noting specific time frames in which to do it. Then have students work in pairs where they talk to each other while doing the task. More learning usually occurs collaboratively than alone. Typically students are going to talk anyway, so have them talk about their learning. The pair stays together for the duration of that task. And if for some reason the student doesn't like you, he/she may like the person with whom he/she is working.

5. **Use a choice/consequence approach to discipline.** In other words, if a student "messes up" after having heard clear expectations of appropriate behavior, simply express your regret that he/she made a poor choice—and quickly and matter-of-factly establish a natural consequence for the student's misstep.

6. **Have students do a simple planning/goal-setting task each day around their work.** It will significantly lessen impulsivity.

7. **Use a contract system to address individual needs, as well as address different times of finishing work.** I did this with ninth-graders. One day a week the students worked independently; it was 20% of their grade. At the beginning of each grading period, I gave them a list of activities they could choose from. Each activity had points assigned to it, and the student was to identify 100 points toward which he/she would work. The students divided the activities by week and

identified what they would finish each week. If a student was particularly weak in a certain area, I would tell him/her to get some points from that area. If a student finished early, I would say, "Go work on your contract." That way students were always busy and always learning.

8. **Separate students who must be separated.** Talk to your administrator about any student combinations that are problematic together and arrange to have them placed in different classrooms.

CONCLUSION

Learning involves both the physical (the brain) and the environmental influences (the mind). For students who haven't had much exposure to the abstract or to representational systems, they are new learners to the abstract. As new learners, they need three things: the how, the why, and the what. Then they can begin patterning information in order to use it in the long term. Since patterns seem to be related to the structure of the subject matter, it's important to teach mental models.

Because virtually all learning involves emotion, relationships of mutual respect energize, at the most basic level, the motivation to learn.

To close with our computer analogy, the hardware (the brain) needs the software (the mind) to function. Nothing functions without the person at the keyboard or the individual giving voice commands—just as next to nothing in learning occurs without relationships of mutual respect.

BIBLIOGRAPHY

Achievement in America 2000. (2001). Retrieved October 2007 from http://www.edtrust.org

Allee, V. (1997). *The knowledge evolution: Building organizational intelligence.* Newton, MA: Butterworth-Heinemann.

Anderson, J. R. (1996). *The architecture of cognition.* Mahwah, NJ: Erlbaum.

Berliner, D. C. (1988, October). *Implications of studies of expertise in pedagogy for teacher education and evaluation.* Paper presented at Educational Testing Service Invitational Conference on New Directions for Teacher Assessment, New York.

Biemiller, A. (2000). Vocabulary: The missing link between phonics and comprehension. *Perspectives, 26*(4), 26–30.

Bloom, B. (1976). *Human characteristics and school learning.* New York: McGraw-Hill.

Brandt, R. (1988). On assessment of teaching: A conversation with Lee Shulman. *Educational Leadership, 46*(3), 42–46.

Bransford, J. D., Brown, A. L., & Cocking, R. R. (Eds.). (1999). *How people learn: Brain, mind, experience and school.* Washington, DC: National Academy Press.

Caine, R. N., & Caine, G. (1991). *Making connections: Teaching and the human brain.* Alexandria, VA: Association for Supervision and Curriculum Development.

Caine, R. N., & Caine, G. (1997). *Education on the edge of possibility.* Alexandria, VA: Association for Supervision and Curriculum Development.

Coles, R. (1989). *The call of stories: Teaching and the moral imagination.* Boston: Houghton Mifflin.

Costa, A., & Garmston, R. (1986). *The art of cognitive coaching: Supervision for intelligent teaching.* Sacramento, CA: California State University Press.

Covey, S. R. (1989). *The 7 habits of highly effective people: Powerful lessons in personal change.* New York: Free Press.

Crowell, S. (1989). A new way of thinking: The challenge of the future. Educational *Leadership, 7*(1), 60–63.

Damasio, A. R. (1994). *Descartes' error: Emotion, reason, and the human brain.* New York: G. P. Putnam's Sons.

DeSoto, H. (2000). *The mystery of capital.* New York: Basic Books.

Edvinsson, L., & Malone, M. S. (1997). *Intellectual capital: Realizing your company's true value by finding its hidden brainpower.* New York: HarperCollins.

Egan, K. (1986). *Teaching as story telling.* Chicago: University of Chicago Press.

Egan, K. (1989). Memory, imagination, and learning: Connected by the story. *Phi Delta Kappan, 70*(6), 455–459.

Fassler, D. G., & Dumas, L. S. (1997). *Help me, I'm sad.* New York: Penguin.

Feuerstein, R., Rand, Y., Hoffman, M., & Miller, R. (1980). *Instrumental enrichment: An intervention program for cognitive modifiability.* Baltimore: University Park Press.

Freire, P. (2000). *Pedagogy of the oppressed: 30th anniversary edition.* New York: Continuum International Publishing Group.

Gladwell, M. (2000). *The tipping point: How little things make a big difference.* New York: Little, Brown.

Glickman, C. D. (1990). *Supervision of instruction: A developmental approach* (2nd ed.). Boston: Allyn & Bacon.

Goleman, D. (1995). *Emotional intelligence: Why it can matter more than IQ.* New York: Bantam Books.

Good, T. L., & Brophy, J. E. (1991). *Looking in classrooms* (5th ed.). New York: HarperCollins.

Greene, V. E., & Enfield, M. L. (2004). *Framing your thoughts: Written expression* (Rev. ed.). Bloomington, MN: Language Circle Enterprises.

Greenspan, S. I., & Benderly, B. L. (1997). *The growth of the mind and the endangered origins of intelligence.* Reading, MA: Perseus Books.

Harrison, L. E., & Huntington, S. P. (Eds.). (2000). *Culture matters: How values shape human progress.* New York: Basic Books.

Hart, B., & Risley, T. R. (1995). *Meaningful differences in the everyday experience of young American children.* Baltimore: Paul H. Brookes.

Hock, D. (1999). *Birth of the chaordic age.* San Francisco: Berrett-Koehler.

Howard, P. J. (2000). *The owner's manual for the brain* (2nd ed.). Austin, TX: Bard Press.

Hunter, M. (1982). *Mastery teaching.* El Segundo, CA: TIP Publications.

Idol, L., & Jones, B. F. (Eds.). (1991). *Educational values and cognitive instruction: Implications for reform.* Mahwah, NJ: Erlbaum.

Jensen, E. (1994). *The learning brain.* Del Mar, CA: Turning Point.

Jones, B. F., Pierce, J., & Hunter, B. (1988). Teaching students to construct graphic representations. *Educational Leadership, 46*(4), 20–25.

Jordan, H., Mendro, R., & Weerasinghe, D. (1997, July). *Teacher effects on longitudinal student achievement: A report on research in progress.* Retrieved June 16, 2009, from http://www.dallasisd.org/inside_disd/depts/evalacct/ research/articles/Jordan-Teacher-Effects-on-Longitudinal-Student-Achievement-1997.pdf

Joyce, B., & Showers, B. (1988). *Student achievement through staff development.* New York: Longman.

Joyce, B., & Weil, M. (1986). *Models of teaching* (3rd ed.). Boston: Allyn & Bacon.

Marzano, R. J., & Arredondo, D. (1986). *Tactics for thinking.* Aurora, CO: Mid-Continent Regional Educational Laboratory.

McCarthy, B. (1996). *About learning.* Barrington, IL: Excel.

McTighe, J., & Lyman, F. T., Jr. (1988). Cueing thinking in the classroom: The promise of theory-embedded tools. *Educational Leadership, 45*(7), 18–24.

O'Dell, C., & Grayson, J. C., Jr., with Essaides, N. (1998). *If only we knew what we know.* New York: Free Press.

Oshry, B. (1995). Seeing systems: *Unlocking the mysteries of organizational life.* San Francisco: Berrett-Koehler.

Palincsar, A. S., & Brown, A. L. (1984). The reciprocal teaching of comprehension-fostering and comprehension-monitoring activities. *Cognition and Instruction, 1*(2), 117–175.

Porter, A. C., & Brophy, J. (1988). Synthesis of research on good teaching: Insights from the work of the Institute for Research on Teaching. *Educational Leadership, 45*(8), 74–85.

Resnick, L. B., & Klopfer, L. (Eds.). (1989). *Toward the thinking curriculum: Current cognitive research.* Alexandria, VA: Association for Supervision and Curriculum Development.

Ridley, M. (2000). *Genome: The autobiography of a species in 23 chapters.* New York: HarperCollins.

Rieber, R. W. (Ed.). (1997). *The collected works of L. S. Vygotsky: Vol. 4. The history of the development of higher mental functions.* New York: Plenum Press.

Rosenholtz, S. J. (1989). *Teachers' workplace: The social organization of schools.* New York: Longman.

Sanders, W. L., & Rivers, J. C. (1996). Cumulative and residual effects of teachers on future student academic achievement. Retrieved May 21, 2009, from http://www.mccsc.edu/~curriculum/cumulative%20and%20residual%20effects%20of%20teachers.pdf

Sapolsky, R. M. (1998). *Why zebras don't get ulcers.* New York: W. H. Freeman.

Senge, P., McCabe, N. H. C., Lucas, T., Kleiner, A., Dutton, J., & Smith, B. (2000). *Schools that learn: A fifth discipline fieldbook for educators, parents, and everyone who cares about education.* New York: Broadway Business.

Senge, P., Ross, R., Smith, B., Roberts, C., & Kleiner, A. (1994). *The fifth discipline fieldbook: Strategies and tools for building a learning organization.* New York: Doubleday-Currency.

Sharron, H., & Coulter, M. (2004). *Changing children's minds: Feuerstein's revolution in the teaching of intelligence.* Highlands, TX: aha! Process.

Shulman, L. S. (1987). Assessment for teaching: An initiative for the profession. *Phi Delta Kappan, 69*(1), 38–44.

Shulman, L. S. (1988). A union of insufficiencies: Strategies for teacher assessment in a period of educational reform. *Educational Leadership, 46*(3), 36–41.

Stewart, T. A. (1997). *Intellectual capital: The new wealth of organizations.* New York: Doubleday-Currency.

Sveiby, K. E. (1997). *The new organizational wealth: Managing and measuring knowledge-based assets.* San Francisco: Berrett-Koehler.

Walberg, H. J. (1990). Productive teaching and instruction: Assessing the knowledge base. *Phi Delta Kappan, 71*(6), 470–478.

Watson, B., & Konicek, R. (1990). Teaching for conceptual change: Confronting children's experience. *Phi Delta Kappan, 71*(9), 680–685.

Wiggins, G., & McTighe, J. (1998). *Understanding by design.* Alexandria, VA: Association for Supervision and Curriculum Development.

Wilson, E. O. (1998). *Consilience: The unity of knowledge.* New York: Alfred A. Knopf.

Wise, A. (1995). *The high performance mind: Mastering brainwaves for insight, healing, and creativity.* New York: Tarcher/Putnam.

Wong, H. K., & Wong, R. T. (1998). *The first day of school: How to be an effective teacher* (Rev. ed.). Mountainview, CA: Author.

RESEARCH ON THE BRAINS OF CHILDREN IN POVERTY USING EEG SCANS

University of California, Berkeley, did research using EEG scans to compare the brains of poor children ages 9 and 10 with middle-class children (*Journal of Cognitive Neuroscience*, 2009). Mark Kishiyama, lead researcher, indicated that the brain patterns in children from poverty were quite similar to adults who have had strokes and therefore have lesions in their prefrontal cortex. The study asked the children to push a button when a tilted triangle appeared. Most low-income children had difficulty identifying the tilted triangle and blocking out the distractions, which is a key function of the prefrontal cortex. The study found that these effects are reversible but need highly intensive interventions.

What additional studies have found is that most low-income children have these disparities in neurocognitive development: language, memory ability, working memory, and executive function (Farah et al., 2006). However, visual and spatial cognitive ability did not differ significantly from middle-class children.

What does the prefrontal part of the brain do? It is the site of the executive function and working memory. Farah et al. (2006) define the prefrontal executive system as doing three things: (1) working memory ("hold information 'online' and maintain it over an interval and manipulate it"), (2) cognitive control ("resist the routine or most easily available response in favor of a more task-appropriate response"), and (3) reward processing ("regulating our responses in the face of rewarding stimuli ... resisting the immediate pull of an attractive stimulus to maximize more long-term gains"). What the executive system does is impact behavioral self-regulation, adult intelligence, and problem-solving ability (Davis et al., 2002; Duncan et al., 1995; Engle et al., 1999; Gray et al., 2003).

Furthermore, research at Cornell University researched 339 poor children in upstate rural New York from 1997 to 2006. Ninety-seven percent of these children were Caucasian. "The findings suggest that poverty, over the course of childhood and early adolescence increases allostatic load, and this dysregulation, in turn, explains some of the subsequent deficits in working memory four years later" (Schamberg, 2008). The allostatic load, as noted previously, is the adjustments of the human body's neuroendocrine, nervous, cardiovascular, metabolic, and immune systems to the demands of the environment. The more stressful the environment, the greater the dysregulation of the system. Because poverty environments are so stressful and unstable, the constant adjustments impact working memory by increasing the allostatic load. The greater the allostatic load, the less the working memory system functions—particularly for non-survival tasks.

Examples of working memory/executive function in the classroom would include the following:

- Giving multiple directions at once and the student being unable to follow them
- Planning
- Task completion
- Behavioral self-regulation
- Ability to identify options

In short, it is most of the input strategies as identified by Feuerstein.

What Does This Mean in Practice?

1. We have to teach students to plan (executive function).
2. Visual images can be used to translate to new ideas using mental models. Visual imaging capability is not impacted by poverty.
3. Direct-teach the input strategies through games and classroom activities.
4. Vocabulary acquisition can be taught by using sketching, a visual activity.
5. Procedural processes using step sheets can be taught to develop executive function.
6. Mediate all learning by teaching the what (vocabulary), the why (meaning and relevance), and the how (the process: executive function).
7. Have students make a plan for their behavior, then give them rewards based upon their ability to meet their own plan. Each plan includes an academic goal and a behavioral goal.
8. Details (executive function) are assisted through visuals and step sheets.
9. Well-organized, non-chaotic schools and classrooms reduce allostatic load. Classroom management is a must because it allows working memory to function better.
10. Use visuals to translate from the sensory to the abstract representational world of paper, ideas, number, letter, drawings, etc.
11. Question making is a key function in problem solving (executive function). Teach students to develop their own multiple-choice questions.

WHAT DOES THE RESEARCH SAY ABOUT INTERGENERATIONAL TRANSFER OF KNOWLEDGE?

Intergenerational transfer of knowledge has been documented in the research. A study done in Australia followed more than 8,500 children for 14 years—from the first clinic visit for pregnancy to age 14 (Najman et al., 2004). The study found that the occupational status of the child's maternal grandfather independently predicted the child's verbal comprehension levels at age 5 and the nonverbal reasoning scores at age 14.

Why would the maternal grandfather's occupation be so predictive? The occupation would tell you the level of stability in the household and be a predictor of the level of education in the family. Because the mother is so instrumental in the early nurturing of the child and the vocabulary that the child hears, it would follow that the mother's access to knowledge and vocabulary would be based on her own childhood experiences; thus the maternal grandfather's occupation would be instrumental in predicting achievement. A U.S. study by Hart and Risley (1995) found that a 3-year-old in a professional household has more vocabulary than an adult in a welfare household.

It would be very easy for educators to now dismiss any attempt to educate children by saying, in effect, "Well, it depends on what their grandfather did." But someone taught the grandfather, and someone taught the mother. Therefore, current educators can impact two generations through the students they have in their classrooms and through parent training.

The key issues here are language acquisition and the development of the prefrontal/executive functions of the brain.

What Does This Mean in Practice?

1. You cannot teach what you do not know. Parent training for parents in poverty should be about human capacity development of the adult—i.e., giving adults language to talk about their own experience, having adults develop their own future story, teaching adults to plan and ask questions, teaching them how to analyze and leverage their own resources, and teaching them to build their own literacy base by recording their personal stories (see *Getting Ahead in a Just-Gettin'-By World*: www.ahaprocess.com).

2. To decrease allostatic load in adults, it is important to give them the tools—planning, resource analysis, problem solving, etc.—that will make their lives less stressful. These are all tools that are part of prefrontal/executive function. If the adult came from generational poverty, chances are these brain functions are not well developed for him/her as well.

LEVELS OF PROCESSING

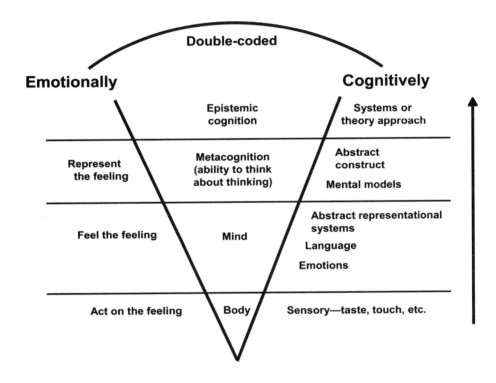

This diagram shows what separates the body, the mind, the ability to think, and the ability to analyze. What separates the body from the mind are emotions; what separates the mind from metacognition (ability to think) are mental models or abstract representations; what separates metacognition (ability to think) from epistemic cognition is the ability to analyze the framework or the theoretical structure of one's thinking.

Payne (2005b) elaborates using the example of a welder. At the body level, he or she welds. This level involves the senses—vision and touch, in this example—and the person acts on his or her senses/feelings. At the next level, the mind, the welder can talk about welding and feel the feeling that comes with a job well done. At the mind level, the welder uses language to express feelings and thoughts, and at metacognition he or she welds against a blueprint. At the level of epistemic cognition, the welder can assess blueprints for structural strength. A systems approach or theory approach is involved.

SITUATED LEARNING

In the research on "situated learning" (Lave and Wenger, 1991), the authors reveal "how different schooling is from the activities and culture that give meaning and purpose to what students learn elsewhere." Lave and Wenger focus on the behavior of JPFs (just plain folks) and record that the ways they learn are quite distinct from what students are asked to do (Brown, Collins, and Duguid, 1989).

	Just plain folks	Student	Practicing individual or apprentice
Reason with	Casual stories	Laws	Casual models
Act on	Situations	Symbols	Conceptual situations
Resolve	Emergent problems and dilemmas	Well-defined problems	Ill-defined problems
Produce	Negotiable meaning and socially constructed understanding	Fixed meaning and immutable concepts	Negotiable meaning and socially constructed understanding

Source: "Situated Cognition and the Culture of Learning" by John Seely Brown, Allan Collins, and Paul Duguid. *Educational Researcher*. Vol. 18, No. 1. January-February 1989. pp. 32–42.

Situated-learning research further indicates that the learning occurs in a context within a set of relationships and cultural norms. Lave and Wenger state that for newcomers to the group "the purpose is not to learn *from* talk as a substitute for legitimate peripheral participation; it is to learn *to* talk as a key to legitimate peripheral participation" (1991, pages 108–109). Wenger (1999, pages 73–84) adds that this participation creates a *shared repertoire* of communal resources, which he defines as routines, behaviors, vocabulary, etc.

In other words, hidden rules come out of the environment and are situated in context, culture, and relationships. Furthermore, in the situated-learning approach, learning is always contextualized and relationship-based. School learning, on the other hand, is decontextualized and abstract (on paper, devoid of immediate relationships, using generalized representations).

Rubric for Analysis of Point of View
(highlight the indicators that apply to the story)

SELECTED STORY	USE OF DIALOGUE	USE OF STORY STRUCTURE	USE OF WORD CHOICE	USE OF CHARACTER DEVELOPMENT	PLOT OR CHARACTER OMISSIONS	TELLER
Story A	Dialogue used to develop plot Dialogue used to develop character (i.e., indicate intelligence) Dialogue used to convey feelings	Story starts in middle and uses flashbacks Story uses chronological order (in time) Story is story within story Story is stream of consciousness Episodic story structure (series of situations involving one character)	Words often used to convey feelings Words used to convey action Words used to describe Word choice is angry, happy, bitter, _____ Use of pronouns (I, we, she)	Main character developed through interactions with other characters Main character developed through dialogue about main character Main character developed through situations Main character developed through conflicts Main character developed through absence	What is *not* in dialogue about main character Key scenes that are only referenced or omitted Accuracy of character comments about self or others Story told by only one person	Told in third person Told in first person Told through dreams Told as retelling Told in present tense Told in past tense
Story B	Dialogue used to develop plot Dialogue used to develop character (i.e., indicate intelligence) Dialogue used to convey feelings	Story starts in middle and uses flashbacks Story uses chronological order (in time) Story is story within story Story is stream of consciousness Episodic story structure (series of situations involving one character)	Words often used to convey feelings Words used to convey action Words used to describe Word choice is angry, happy, bitter, _____ Use of pronouns (I, we, she)	Main character developed through interactions with other characters Main character developed through dialogue about main character Main character developed through situations Main character developed through conflicts Main character developed through absence	What is *not* in dialogue about main character Key scenes that are only referenced or omitted Accuracy of character comments about self or others Story told by only one person	Told in third person Told in first person Told through dreams Told as retelling Told in present tense Told in past tense

by aha! Process

ADVANCE
SCHOOL IMPROVEMENT

Advance: School Improvement

Teacher-friendly. Collegial. Highly collaborative. Simpler processes that take less time and money.

These are all phrases that describe Advance: School Improvement. As more and more schools face the consequences of not making the required growth in student achievement, a simpler yet comprehensive model is required. The work of Dr. Ruby K. Payne and her colleagues provides such a model, which has been used for nearly a decade. Results have shown that when the model is implemented with fidelity, student achievement increases and achievement gaps have even been narrowed at some sites.

Processes and Applications

Advance is comprised of nine processes to raise achievement in high poverty schools. Each process has specific classroom applications aligned to the process that can be monitored by the school leader. The result is artifacts that reflect the processes, along with applications that extend strategies into the classroom.

The processes apply to all levels of schools, beginning with 4-year-olds and continuing through Grade 12. These processes are embedded with the assistance of an academic coach (aha! consultant or district/building instructional coach) in two-hour increments, after the foundational workshops. Foundational workshops include: A Framework for Understanding Poverty, Research-Based Strategies, and Raising Achievement with 9 Systemic Processes. The nine processes that actually comprise Advance:

1. Gridding student data
2. Developing time and content grids, based on the standards and students' needs
3. Understanding assessment context, state assessment glossary, academic vocabulary, and the assessment blueprint
4. Developing 10-question tests that measure students' progress against the standards for the first semester
5. Identifying interventions based on analysis of 10-question tests and analyzing grade distribution or failure/passing rate

6. Understanding content comprehension and incorporating processes, step sheets, planning, and mental models into lessons; response to intervention also is addressed in this step
7. Developing 10-question tests for the second semester
8. Calibrating curriculum and completing artifact analyses using rubrics
9. Reviewing adult voice, putting students in charge of their own learning, and relational learning for students, including technology integration

Because these processes provide scaffolding for instruction, they are deliberately designed for delivery in the order outlined. The gridding of data identified as the first process is a mandatory step that must be completed by teachers when working with Advance. We realize that districts and schools have a great deal of data available to them and may have a process in place to disaggregate data, but our experience has been that unless the teachers themselves work through this first process, they seldom truly understand the implications of the data and the needs of the students with whom they are working. Many are not comfortable analyzing data and knowing how to use it effectively. They can be described as "data rich, but information poor" (Ronka, Lachat, Slaughter, & Meltzer, 2008, 2009). As you work through the processes, you also will find that teachers are being asked to work in learning communities, to share best practices, and to support and work with one another. The professional dialog that occurs during these sessions can profoundly shape the culture of a building and the relationships of the adults who work together in it.

It is our hope that Advance will inspire you in your process of change, that you will adapt it for your needs, and that you will focus on continuous improvement as you work with the strategies and refine and improve on them over the years.

With Advance: School Improvement, you will find that all of the processes could be completed by a grade level or department in a three-day period—or the work can be spread out over the school year, allowing teachers time to work with the processes before adding the next step. The decision is yours. Our desire is to provide the flexibility and ease of use while helping you to meet your accountability goals, build capacity of your staff, and provide a model that can be sustained over a period of time. For more information, contact Dr. Donna Magee at (800) 424-9484.

Advance: School Improvement

	Process	Classroom Application
2 hours	Data analysis	Math—problem-solving model ELA—nonfiction reading strategy and open-response strategy Share examples of walk-throughs
2 hours	Assigning time, aligning instruction *	Bellwork
2 hours	Assessment context, state assessment glossary, academic vocabulary, assessment blueprint	Word wall, vocabulary sketching (mental models) (Consultant needs time scheduled with principal to review assessment blueprint)
2 hours	Ten-question tests—first semester: reading, writing, math	Examples of mental models
2 hours	Interventions, data analysis, grade distribution, failure rate	Resource analysis and interventions
2 hours	Content comprehension—processes, step sheets, planning, RTI, specific mental models	Research-based strategies and targeted interventions using intervention form
2 hours	Ten-question tests—second semester: reading, writing, math	Question making
2 hours	Curriculum calibration, artifacts analysis, rubrics	Rubrics: ELA teachers teach writing rubric and open-response rubric to entire staff
2 hours	Voice, putting students in charge of their own learning, relational learning	Data conferencing with students Monitor for use of adult voice in classroom Monitor for examples of relational learning

* Needs to be done for each content area

Foundational Workshops
A Framework for Understanding Poverty
Research-Based Strategies
Raising Achievement with 9 Systemic Processes

Additional Offerings
* Curriculum alignment, beyond the development of the time and content grids
* Observation days
* Follow-up with new teachers with the consultant (use certified trainer for foundational trainings)

Required Texts
A Framework for Understanding Poverty
Research-Based Strategies
School Improvement: 9 Systemic Processes to Raise Achievement

Recommended Texts
Putting the Pieces Together (elementary)
Books on secondary mental models

263

BIBLIOGRAPHY

Achievement in America 2000. (2001). Retrieved October 2007 from http://www. edtrust.org

Adelabu, D. H. (2008). Future time perspective, hope, and ethnic identity among African American adolescents. *Urban Education, 43*(3), 347–360.

Adger, C. (1994). *Enhancing the delivery of services to black special education students from non-standard English backgrounds.* (ERIC Document Reproduction Service No. ED370377)

Agran, M., Blanchard, C., Wehmeyer, M., & Hughes, C. (2001). Teaching students to self-regulate their behavior: The differential effects of student- vs. teacher-delivered reinforcement. *Research in Developmental Disabilities, 22*(4), 319–332.

Allee, V. (1997). *The knowledge evolution: Building organizational intelligence.* Newton, MA: Butterworth-Heinemann.

Allen, J. (2004). *Tools for teaching content literacy.* Portland, ME: Stenhouse.

American Psychiatric Association. (1994). *Diagnostic and statistical manual of mental disorders* (4th ed.). Washington, DC: Author.

Amyx, D., & Bristow, D. (2004). Future time orientation and student expectations: An empirical investigation. *Delta Pi Epsilon Journal, 46*(1), 1–17.

Anderson, J. R. (1996). *The architecture of cognition.* Mahwah, NJ: Erlbaum.

Andrade, H. G. (1999a). *The role of instructional rubrics and self-assessment in learning to write: A smorgasbord of findings.* (ERIC Document Reproduction Service No. ED431029)

Andrade, H. G. (1999b). *Student self-assessment: At the intersection of metacognition and authentic assessment.* (ERIC Document Reproduction Service No. ED431030)

Andrade, H. L., Du, Y., & Wang, X. (2008). Putting rubrics to the test: The effect of a model, criteria generation, and rubric-referenced self-assessment on elementary school students' writing. *Educational Measurement, 27*(2), 3–13.

Andreas, S., & Faulkner, C. (Eds.). (1994). NLP: *The new technology of achievement.* New York: William Morrow.

Apperly, I. A., Williams, E., & Williams, J. (2004). Three- to four-year-olds' recognition that symbols have a stable meaning: Pictures are understood before written words. *Child Development, 75*(5), 1510–1522.

April, A. (2001). Toward a finer description of the connection between arts education and student achievement. Arts Education Policy Review, 102(5), 25–26.

The arts and educational reform: Ideas for schools and communities. (1994). (ERIC Document Reproduction Service No. ED365621)

Asbury, C., & Rich, B. (Eds.). (2008). *Learning, arts and the brain: The Dana Consortium report on arts and cognition.* New York: Dana Foundation.

Assisting students struggling with reading: Response to intervention (RtI) and multi-tier intervention in the primary grades. (2009). Retrieved June 15, 2009, from http://ies.ed.gov/ncee/wwc/pdf/practiceguides/rti_reading_pg_021809.pdf

Bagby, J. H., Rudd, L. C., & Woods, M. (2005). The effects of socioeconomic diversity on the language, cognitive and social-emotional development of children from low-income backgrounds. *Early Child Development and Care, 175*(5), 395–405.

Baghban, M. (2007). Scribbles, labels, and stories: The role of drawing in the development of writing. *Young Children, 62*(1), 20–26.

Bailey, M., & others/et al. (1995). *The impact of integrating visuals in an elementary creative writing process.* (ERIC Document Reproduction Service No. ED391492)

Bailey, R., Armour, K., Kirk, D., Jess, M., Pickup, I., & Sandford, R. (2009). The educational benefits claimed for physical education and school sport: An academic review. *Research Papers in Education, 24*(1), 1–27.

Bakunas, B., & Holley, W. (2004). Teaching organizational skills. *Clearing House, 77*(3), 92–97.

Barley, Z., & Beesley, A. D. (2007). Rural school success: What can we learn? *Journal of Research in Rural Education, 22*(1), 1–16.

Barnett, R. C., Gareis, K. C., James, J. B., & Steele, J. (2001). *Planning ahead: College seniors' concerns about work-family conflict.* (ERIC Document Reproduction Service No. ED457506)

Barter, B. (2007). Communities in schools: A Newfoundland school and community outreach in need of stability. *Alberta Journal of Educational Research, 53*(4), 359–372.

Bassuk, E. L., Buckner, J. C., Weinreb, L. F., Browne, A., Bassuk, S., Dawson, R., et al. (1997). Homelessness in female-headed families: Childhood and adult risk and protective factors. *American Journal of Public Health, 87*(2), 241–248.

Beatham, M. D. (2009). Tools of inquiry: Separating tool and task to promote true learning. *Journal of Educational Technology Systems, 37*(1), 61–70.

Becker, K. A., Krodel, K. M., & Tucker, B. H. (2009). *Understanding and engaging under-resourced college students: A fresh look at economic class and its influence on teaching and learning in higher education.* Highlands, TX: aha! Process.

Beers, K. (2003). *When kids can't read: What teachers can do.* Portsmouth, NH: Heinemann.

Beeson, E., & Strange, M. (2003). Why rural matters 2003: The continuing need for every state to take action on rural education. *Journal of Research in Rural Education, 18*(1), 3–16.

Behrmann, M., & Jerome, M. K. (2002). *Assistive technology for students with mild disabilities: Update 2002.* Arlington, VA: ERIC Clearinghouse on Disabilities and Gifted Education, Council for Exceptional Children. (ERIC Document Reproduction Service No. ED463595)

Berliner, D. C. (1988, October). *Implications of studies of expertise in pedagogy for teacher education and evaluation.* Paper presented at Educational Testing Service Invitational Conference on New Directions for Teacher Assessment, New York.

Berne, E. (1996). *Games people play: The basic handbook of transactional analysis.* New York: Ballantine Books.

Berzonsky, M. D., Branje, S. J. T., & Meeus, W. (2007). Identity-processing style, psychosocial resources, and adolescents' perceptions of parent-adolescent relations. *Journal of Early Adolescence, 27*(3), 324–345.

Bianchi, A. J., & Lancianese, D. A. (2005). No child left behind? Role/identity development of the 'good student.' *International Journal of Educational Policy, Research, and Practice, 6*(1), 3–29.

Biemiller, A. (2000). Vocabulary: The missing link between phonics and comprehension. *Perspectives, 26*(4), 26–30.

Billig, S. H. (2002). Support for K–12 service-learning practice: A brief review of the research. *Educational Horizons, 80*(4), 184–189.

Bloom, B. (1976). *Human characteristics and school learning.* New York: McGraw-Hill.

Boulware-Gooden, R., Carreker, S., Thornhill, A., & Joshi, R. M. (2007). Instruction of metacognitive strategies enhances reading comprehension and vocabulary achievement of third-grade students. *Reading Teacher, 61*(1), 70–77.

Bowles, T. (2008). The relationship of time orientation with perceived academic performance and preparation for assessment in adolescents. *Educational Psychology, 28*(5), 551–565.

Brandt, R. (1988). On assessment of teaching: A conversation with Lee Shulman. *Educational Leadership, 46*(3), 42–46.

Bransford, J. D., Brown, A. L., & Cocking, R. R. (Eds.). (1999). *How people learn: Brain, mind, experience and school.* Washington, DC: National Academy Press.

Brink, J., Capps, E., & Sutko, A. (2004). Student exam creation as a learning tool. *College Student Journal, 38*(2), 262–272.

Britsch, B., & Wakefield, W. D. (1998). *The influence of ethnic identity status and gender-role identity on social anxiety and avoidance in Latina adolescents.* (ERIC Document Reproduction Service No. ED442895)

Brooks, R. (1991). *The self-esteem teacher.* Loveland, OH: Treehaus Communications.

Brown, J. S., Collins, A., & Duguid, P. (1989). Situated cognition and the culture of learning. *Educational Researcher, 18*(1), 32–42.

Bruce, C., Snodgrass, D., & Salzman, J. A. (1999). *A tale of two methods: Melding Project Read and guided reading to improve at-risk students' literacy skills.* (ERIC Document Reproduction Service No. ED436762)

Buckner, M., Reese, E., & Reese, R. (1987). Eye movement as an indicator of sensory components in thought. *Journal of Counseling Psychology, 34*(3), 283–287.

Burke, P. J., Owens, T. J., Serpe, R., & Thoits, P. A. (Eds.). (2003). *Advances in identity theory and research.* New York: Springer.

Burton, L. J., & VanHeest, J. L. (2007). The importance of physical activity in closing the achievement gap. *Quest, 59*(2), 212–218.

Burts, D. C., Schmidt, H. M., Durham, R. S., Charlesworth, R., & Hart, C. H. (2007). Impact of the developmental appropriateness of teacher guidance strategies on kindergarten children's interpersonal relations. *Journal of Research in Childhood Education, 21*(3), 290–301.

Butera, L. M., Giacone, M. V., & Wagner, K. A. (2008). *Decreasing off-task behavior through a dot/point reward system and portfolio reflection with second, fifth, and sixth graders.* (ERIC Document Reproduction Service No. ED500845)

Caine Learning Center. (n.d.). Retrieved May 19, 2009, from http://cainelearning.com

Caine, R. N., & Caine, G. (1991). *Making connections: Teaching and the human brain.* Alexandria, VA: Association for Supervision and Curriculum Development.

Caine, R. N., & Caine, G. (1997). *Education on the edge of possibility.* Alexandria, VA: Association for Supervision and Curriculum Development.

Callicott, K. J., & Park, H. (2003). Effects of self-talk on academic engagement and academic responding. *Behavioral Disorders, 29*(1), 48–64.

Campbell, T. (2006). The distant exploration of wolves: Using technology to explore student questions about wolves. *Journal of College Science Teaching, 35*(7), 16–21.

Carrell, P. L. (1987). Content and formal schemata in ESL reading. *TESOL Quarterly, 21*(3), 461–481.

Chagnon, F. (2007). Coping mechanisms, stressful events and suicidal behavior among youth admitted to juvenile justice and child welfare services. *Suicide and Life-Threatening Behavior, 37*(4), 439–452.

Chalk, J. C., Hagan-Burke, S., & Burke, M. D. (2005). The effects of self-regulated strategy development on the writing process for high school students with learning disabilities. *Learning Disability Quarterly, 28*(1), 75–87.

Chalmers, D., & Lawrence, J. A. (1993). Investigating the effects of planning aids on adults' and adolescents' organisation of a complex task. *International Journal of Behavioral Development, 16*(2), 191–214.

Cheung, A., & Slavin, R. E. (2005). Effective reading programs for English language learners and other language-minority students. *Bilingual Research Journal, 29*(2), 241–267.

Child poverty in perspective: An overview of child well-being in rich countries. (2007). Retrieved May 20, 2009, from http://www.unicef.org/media/files/ChildPovertyReport.pdf

Children's Defense Fund Minnesota. (2009). Retrieved May 20, 2009, from http://www.cdf-mn.org

Chin, C., & Kayalvizhi, G. (2002). Posing problems for open investigations: What questions do pupils ask? *Research in Science and Technological Education, 20*(2), 269–87.

Chin, C., & Osborne, J. (2008). Students' questions: A potential resource for teaching and learning science. *Studies in Science Education, 44*(1), 1–39.

Chomitz, V. R., Slining, M. M., McGowan, R. J., Mitchell, S. E., Dawson, G. F., & Hacker, K. A. (2009). Is there a relationship between physical fitness and academic achievement? Positive results from public school children in the Northeastern United States. *Journal of School Health, 79*(1), 30–37.

Cinamon, R. G., & Rich, Y. (2002). Profiles of attribution of importance to life roles and their implications for work-family conflict. *Journal of Counseling Psychology, 49,* 212–220.

Circles Campaign. (2009). Retrieved May 20, 2009, from http://www. movethemountain.org/circlescampaign.aspx

ClassWide Peer Tutoring: What Works Clearinghouse intervention report. (2007). Rockville, MD: What Works Clearinghouse. (ERIC Document Reproduction Service No. ED499239)

Coles, R. (1989). *The call of stories: Teaching and the moral imagination.* Boston: Houghton Mifflin.

Collier, P. J., & Morgan, D. L. (2008). Is that paper really due today? Differences in first-generation and traditional college students' understandings of faculty expectations. *Higher Education, 55*(4), 425–446.

Comer, J. (1995). Lecture given at Education Service Center, Region IV, Houston, TX.

Committee on the Support for Thinking Spatially: The Incorporation of Geographic Information Science Across the K–12 Curriculum, Committee on Geography, National Research Council. (2006). *Learning to think spatially: GIS as a support system in the K–12 curriculum.* Washington, DC: National Academies Press.

Communities in Schools. (2009). Retrieved May 13, 2009, from http://www.cisnet.org/

Conlon, T. (2009). Towards sustainable text concept mapping. *Literacy, 43*(1), 20–28.

Conway, H. W. (2006). *Collaboration for kids: Early-intervention tools for schools and communities.* Highlands, TX: aha! Process.

Costa, A., & Garmston, R. (1986). *The art of cognitive coaching: Supervision for intelligent teaching.* Sacramento, CA: California State University Press.

Covey, S. R. (1989). *The 7 habits of highly effective people: Powerful lessons in personal change.* New York: Free Press.

Cox, H. A., & Stephens, L. J. (2006). The effect of music participation on mathematical achievement and overall academic achievement of high school students. *International Journal of Mathematical Education in Science and Technology, 37*(7), 757–763.

Coyle, C., & Cole, P. (2004). A videotaped self-modeling and self-monitoring treatment program to decrease off-task behaviour in children with autism. *Journal of Intellectual and Developmental Disability, 29*(1), 3–16.

Crowell, S. (1989). A new way of thinking: The challenge of the future. *Educational Leadership, 7*(1), 60–63.

Daly, M. & Valletta, R. (2004). *Inequality and poverty in the United States: The effects of rising male wage dispersion and changing family behavior.* Retrieved May 20, 2009, from http://www.frbsf.org/econrsrch/workingp/2000/wp00-06.pdf

Damasio, A. R. (1994). *Descartes' error: Emotion, reason, and the human brain.* New York: G. P. Putnam's Sons.

del Mar Badia Martin, M., Gotzens Busquet, C., Genovard Rossello, C., & Castelló Tarrida, A. (2007). Formulation of 'questions-answers' in teaching-learning process as a way of improving learning of students at university level. Retrieved June 10, 2009, from http://www.academicleadership.org/emprical_research/Formulation_of_questions.shtml

Dermody, M. M., & Speaker, R. B., Jr. (1999). Reciprocal strategy training in prediction, clarification, question generating and summarization to improve reading comprehension. *Reading Improvement, 36*(1), 16–23.

DeSoto, H. (2000). *The mystery of capital.* New York: Basic Books.

Desrochers, S. (2002). *Predicting work-family role strain among business professors from their identity-based and time-based commitments to professional and parenting roles. BLCC Working Paper #02–05.* Available from http://www.human.cornell.edu/che/BLCC/Research/Publications/workingpapers.cfm

DeVol, P. E. (2006). *Getting ahead in a just-gettin'-by world: Building your resources for a better life.* (2nd ed.). Highlands, TX: aha! Process.

DeVol, P. E., Payne, R. K., & Smith, T. D. (2006). *Bridges out of poverty: Strategies for professionals and communities workbook.* Highlands, TX: aha! Process.

DeWitz, S. J., Woolsey, M. L., & Walsh, W. B. (2009). College student retention: An exploration of the relationship between self-efficacy beliefs and purpose in life among college students. *Journal of College Student Development, 50*(1), 19–34.

Diaconis, P., & Mosteller, F. (1989). Methods of studying coincidences. *Journal of the American Statistical Association, 84*(408), 853–861.

Diemer, M. A. (2002). Constructions of provider role identity among African American men: An exploratory study. *Cultural Diversity and Ethnic Minority Psychology, 8*(1), 30–40.

Domagala-Zysk, E. (2006). The significance of adolescents' relationships with significant others and school failure. *School Psychology International, 27*(2), 232–247.

Donovan, M. S., & Bransford, J. D. (2005). *How students learn: History, mathematics, and science in the classroom.* Washington, DC: National Academies Press.

Dweck, C. (2006). *Mindset: The new psychology of success.* New York: Ballantine Books.

Edvinsson, L., & Malone, M. S. (1997). *Intellectual capital: Realizing your company's true value by finding its hidden brainpower.* New York: HarperCollins.

Egan, K. (1986). *Teaching as story telling.* Chicago: University of Chicago Press.

Egan, K. (1989). Memory, imagination, and learning: Connected by the story. *Phi Delta Kappan, 70*(6), 455–459.

Elliott, M., Gray, B., & Lewicki, R. (2003). Lessons learned about the framing of intractable environmental conflicts. In R. Lewicki, B. Gray, & M. Elliott (Eds.), *Making sense of intractable environmental conflicts: Concepts and cases* (pp. 409–436), Washington, DC: Island Press.

Elliott, M., Kaufman, S., Gardner, R., & Burgess, G. (2002). Teaching conflict assessment and frame analysis through interactive web-based simulations. *The International Journal of Conflict Management, 13*(4), 320–340.

Ellis, K. E. (2004). *Putting the pieces together.* Highlands, TX: aha! Process.

Ericsson, I. (2008). Motor skills, attention and academic achievements: An intervention study in school years 1–3. *British Educational Research Journal, 34*(3), 301–313.

Evans, P. (1992). *The verbally abusive relationship: How to recognize it and how to respond.* Cincinnati, OH: Adams Media.

Evertson, C. M., & Weinstein, C. S. (Eds.). (2006). *Handbook of classroom management: Research, practice, and contemporary issues.* Mahwah, NJ: Erlbaum.

Eye-openers. (2009). Retrieved May 19, 2009, from http://www.ahaprocess.com

Fain, T., Turner, S., & Ridgeway, G. (2008). *Los Angeles County Juvenile Justice Crime Prevention Act: RAND quarterly report, October 2008.* Santa Monica, CA: RAND Corporation.

Faircloth, B. S., & Hamm, J. V. (2005). Sense of belonging among high school students representing four ethnic groups. *Journal of Youth and Adolescence, 34*(4), 293–309.

Farah, M. J., Noble, K. G., & Hurt, H. (2006). *Poverty, privilege, and brain development: Empirical findings and ethical implications.* Retrieved May 20, 2009, from http://www.psych.upenn.edu/~mfarah/farah_SES_05.pdf

Farah, M. J., Shera, D. M., Savage, J. H., Betancourt, L., Giannetta, J. M., Brodsky, N. L., et al. (2006). Childhood poverty: Specific associations with neurocognitive development. *Brain Research, 1110*(1), 166–174.

Farbman, D., & Kaplan, C. (2005). *Time for a change: The promise of extended time schools for promoting student achievement.* Boston: Massachusetts 2020.

Farmer, T. W., Dadisman, K., Latendresse, S. J., Thompson, J., Irvin, M. J., & Zhang, L. (2006). *Educating out and giving back: Adults' conceptions of successful outcomes of African American high school students from impoverished rural communities.* Retrieved June 10, 2009, from http://www.umaine.edu/jrre/archive/21-10.pdf

Farmer-Hinton, R. L. (2002). *When time matters: Examining the impact and distribution of extra instructional time.* (ERIC Document Reproduction Service No. ED479926)

Farrell, A. D., Erwin, E. H., Allison, K. W., Meyer, A., Sullivan, T., Camou, S., et al. (2007). Problematic situations in the lives of urban African American middle school students: A qualitative study. *Journal of Research on Adolescence, 17*(2), 413–454.

Fassler, D. G., & Dumas, L. S. (1997). *Help me, I'm sad.* New York: Penguin.

Feeney, T. J., & Ylvisaker, M. (2008). Context-sensitive cognitive-behavioral supports for young children with TBI: A second replication study. *Journal of Positive Behavior Interventions, 10*(2), 115–128.

Ferguson, R. (2008). *Toward excellence with equity: An emerging vision for closing the achievement gap.* Cambridge, MA: Harvard Education Press.

Fernyhough, C., & Fradley, E. (2005). Private speech on an executive task: Relations with task difficulty and task performance. *Cognitive Development, 20*(1), 103–120.

Feuerstein, R. (1998). *Glossary of MLE, LPAD and IE terms and concepts.* Jerusalem: International Center for the Enhancement of Learning Potential.

Feuerstein, R., Rand, Y., Hoffman, M., & Miller, R. (1980). *Instrumental enrichment: An intervention program for cognitive modifiability.* Baltimore: University Park Press.

Fisher, D., Brozo, W., Frey, N., & Ivey, G. (2006). *50 content area strategies for adolescent literacy.* Upper Saddle River, NJ: Prentice Hall.

Fisher, D., & Frey, N. (2008). *Wordwise and content rich: Five essential steps to teaching academic vocabulary.* Portsmouth, NH: Heinemann.

Fisher, R., & Ury, W. (1983). *Getting to YES: Negotiating agreement without giving in.* New York: Penguin.

Fox, J. E. (1999). 'It's time to go home!' Reframing dismissal routines. *Dimensions of Early Childhood, 27*(3), 11–15.

Fraser, M. W., Galinsky, M. J., Smokowski, P. R., Day, S. H., Terzian, M. A., Rose, R. A., et al. (2005). Social information-processing skills training to promote social competence and prevent aggressive behavior in the third grades. *Journal of Consulting and Clinical Psychology, 73*(6), 1045–1055.

Freed, M., Hess, R., & Ryan, J. (Eds.). (2002). *The educator's desk reference: A sourcebook of educational information and research.* Westport, CT: Praeger.

Freedman, J., & Combs, G. (1996). *Narrative therapy: The social construction of preferred realities.* New York: Norton.

Freire, P. (2000). *Pedagogy of the oppressed: 30th anniversary edition.* New York: Continuum International Publishing Group.

Fuchs, L. S., Fuchs, D., Prentice, K., Hamlett, C. L., Finelli, R., & Courey, S. J. (2004). Enhancing mathematical problem solving among third-grade students with schema-based instruction. *Journal of Educational Psychology, 96*(4), 635–647.

Gaddy, S. A., Bakken, J. P., & Fulk, B. M. (2008). The effects of teaching text-structure strategies to postsecondary students with learning disabilities to improve their reading comprehension on expository science text passages. *Journal of Postsecondary Education and Disability, 20*(2), 100–119.

Gajria, M., Jitendra, A. K., Sood, S., & Sacks, G. (2007). Improving comprehension of expository text in students with LD: A research synthesis. *Journal of Learning Disabilities, 40*(3), 210–225.

Galton, M., Hargreaves, L., & Pell, T. (2009). Group work and whole-class teaching with 11- to 14-year-olds compared. *Cambridge Journal of Education, 39*(1), 119–140.

Gambill, J. M., Moss, L. A., & Vescogni, C. D. (2008). *The impact of study skills and organizational methods on student achievement.* (ERIC Document Reproduction Service No. ED501312)

Garcia-Ros, R., Perez-Gonzalez, F., & Hinojosa, E. (2004). Assessing time management skills as an important aspect of student learning: The construction and evaluation of a time management scale with Spanish high school students. *School Psychology International, 25*(2), 167–183.

Gianakos, I. (1995). The relation of sex role identity to career decision-making self-efficacy. *Journal of Vocational Behavior, 46*(2), 131–43.

Gillies, R. M. (2004). The effects of cooperative learning on junior high school students during small group learning. *Learning and Instruction, 14*(2), 197–213.

276

Gillies, R. M. (2008). The effects of cooperative learning on junior high school students' behaviours, discourse and learning during a science-based learning activity. *School Psychology International, 29*(3), 328–347.

Giota, J. (2006). Why am I in school? Relationships between adolescents' goal orientation, academic achievement and self-evaluation. *Scandinavian Journal of Educational Research, 50*(4), 441–461.

Gladwell, M. (2000). *The tipping point: How little things make a big difference.* New York: Little, Brown.

Gladwell, M. (2008). *Outliers: The story of success.* New York: Little, Brown.

Glickman, C. D. (1990). *Supervision of instruction: A developmental approach* (2nd ed.). Boston: Allyn & Bacon.

Goddard, Y. L., & Sendi, C. (2008). Effects of self-monitoring on the narrative and expository writing of four fourth-grade students with learning disabilities. *Reading and Writing Quarterly, 24*(4), 408–433.

Godley, A. J., & Minnici, A. (2008). Critical language pedagogy in an urban high school English class. *Urban Education, 43*(3), 319–346.

Goldratt, E. M. (1990). *Theory of constraints.* Great Barrington, MA: Great River Press.

Goleman, D. (1995). *Emotional intelligence: Why it can matter more than IQ.* New York: Bantam Books.

Goleman, D. (2006). *Social intelligence: The new science of human relationships.* New York: Bantam Books.

Good, M., & Adams, G. R. (2008). Linking academic social environments, ego-identity formation, ego virtues, and academic success. *Adolescence, 43*(170), 221–236.

Good, T. L., & Brophy, J. E. (1991). *Looking in classrooms* (5th ed.). New York: HarperCollins.

Gouzouasis, P., Guhn, M., & Kishor, N. (2007). The predictive relationship between achievement and participation in music and achievement in core grade 12 academic subjects. *Music Education Research, 9*(1), 81–92.

Gredler, M. E. (2004). Games and simulations and their relationships to learning. In D. H. Jonassen (Ed.), *Handbook of research on educational communications and technology* (pp. 571–582). Mahwah, NJ: Erlbaum.

Green, G., Rhodes, J., Hirsch, A. H., Suarez-Orozco, C., & Camic, P. M. (2008). Supportive adult relationships and the academic engagement of Latin American immigrant youth. *Journal of School Psychology, 46*(4), 393–412.

Greene, B. A., & DeBacker, T. K. (2004). Gender and orientations toward the future: Links to motivation. *Educational Psychology Review, 16*(2), 91–120.

Greene, B. A., Miller, R. B., Crowson, H. M., Duke, B. L., & Akey, K. L. (2004). Predicting high school students' cognitive engagement and achievement: Contributions of classroom perceptions and motivation. *Contemporary Educational Psychology, 29*(4), 462–482.

Greene, J. A., Moos, D. C., Azevedo, R., & Winters, F. I. (2008). Exploring differences between gifted and grade-level students' use of self-regulatory learning processes with hypermedia. *Computers and Education, 50*(3), 1069–1083.

Greene, V. E., & Enfield, M. L. (2004). *Framing your thoughts: Written expression* (Rev. ed.). Bloomington, MN: Language Circle Enterprises.

Greenspan, S. I., & Benderly, B. L. (1997). *The growth of the mind and the endangered origins of intelligence.* Reading, MA: Perseus Books.

Grigsby, B. L. (2005). *African American male students' perceptions of social, emotional, physical, and academic variables in their transition from elementary school to middle school.* Unpublished doctoral dissertation, Texas A&M University, College Station.

Guastello, E. F., Beasley, T. M., & Sinatra, R. C. (2000). Concept mapping effects on science content comprehension of low achieving inner-city seventh graders. *Remedial and Special Education, 21*(6), 356–364.

Guay, F., Marsh, H. W., Senecal, C., & Dowson, M. (2008). Representations of relatedness with parents and friends and autonomous academic motivation during the late adolescence-early adulthood period: Reciprocal or unidirectional effects? *British Journal of Educational Psychology, 78*(4), 621–637.

Gunzelmann, G. (2008). Strategy generalization across orientation tasks: Testing a computational cognitive model. *Cognitive Science, 32*(5), 835–861.

Gyselinck, V., Meneghetti, C., De Beni, R., & Pazzaglia, F. (2009). The role of working memory in spatial text processing: What benefit of imagery strategy and visuospatial abilities? *Learning and Individual Differences, 19*(1), 12–20.

Haager, D., Klingner, J., & Vaughn, S. (Eds.). (2007). *Evidence-based reading practices for response to intervention.* Baltimore: Paul H. Brookes.

Hafner, J. C., & Hafner, P. M. (2003). Quantitative analysis of the rubric as an assessment tool: An empirical study of student peer-group rating. *International Journal of Science Education, 25*(12), 1509–1528.

Hagaman, J. L., & Reid, R. (2008). The effects of the paraphrasing strategy on the reading comprehension of middle school students at risk for failure in reading. *Remedial and Special Education, 29*(4), 222–234.

Hall, K. M., Sabey, B. L., & McClellan, M. (2005). Expository text comprehension: Helping primary-grade teachers use expository texts to full advantage. *Reading Psychology, 26*(3), 211–234.

Hamilton, J. L. (2007). *The use of self-management skills with kindergarten through third grade students with emotional and behavior disorders: Investigation of findings.* (ERIC Document Reproduction Service No. ED497000)

Hammond, C., Linton, D., Smink, J., & Drew, S. (2007). *Dropout risk factors and exemplary programs: A technical report.* Clemson, SC: National Dropout Prevention Center/Network.

Harris, M. (2008). The effects of music instruction on learning in the Montessori classroom. *Montessori Life, 20*(3), 24–31.

Harrison, L. E., & Huntington, S. P. (Eds.). (2000). *Culture matters: How values shape human progress.* New York: Basic Books.

Hart, B., & Risley, T. R. (1995). *Meaningful differences in the everyday experience of young American children.* Baltimore: Paul H. Brookes.

Haskitz, A. (1996). A community service program that can be validated. *Phi Delta Kappan, 78*(2), 163–164.

Heath, S. B. (2001). Three's not a crowd: Plans, roles, and focus in the arts. *Educational Researcher, 30*(7), 10–17.

Herman, T., Colton, S., & Franzen, M. (2008). Rethinking outreach: Teaching the process of science through modeling. *PLoS Biol 6*(4), e86. DOI: 10.1371/journal.pbio.0060086

Hill, H. C., Blunk, M. L., Charalambous, Y., Lewis, J. M., Phelps, G. C., Sleep, L., et al. (2008). Mathematical knowledge for teaching and the mathematical quality of instruction: An exploratory study. *Cognition and Instruction, 26*(4), 430–511.

Hock, D. (1999). *Birth of the chaordic age.* San Francisco: Berrett-Koehler.

Hock, M., & Mellard, D. (2005). Reading comprehension strategies for adult literacy outcomes. *Journal of Adolescent and Adult Literacy, 49*(3), 192–200.

Hoffman, A. (2003). *Teaching decision making to students with learning disabilities by promoting self-determination.* Arlington, VA: ERIC Clearinghouse on Disabilities and Gifted Education. (ERIC Document Reproduction Service No. ED481859)

Hollingsworth, J., & Ybarra, S. (2000). *Analyzing classroom instruction: Curriculum calibration.* Retrieved October 2007 from http://www.dataworks-ed.com

Horstmanshof, L., & Zimitat, C. (2007). Future time orientation predicts academic engagement among first-year university students. *British Journal of Educational Psychology, 77*(3), 703–718.

Howard, P. J. (2000). *The owner's manual for the brain* (2nd ed.). Austin, TX: Bard Press.

Hsu, J. (2008). *The secrets of storytelling: Why we love a good yarn.* Retrieved May 20, 2009, from http://www.scientificamerican.com/article.cfm?id=the-secrets-of-storytelling

Huan, V. S. (2006). The role of social and personal identities among at-risk and non-at-risk Singapore youths during peer mediation. *Education Journal, 34*(2), 97–113.

Huang, J., Maassen van den Brink, H., & Groot, W. (in press). A meta-analysis of the effect of education on social capital. *Economics of Education Review.*

Hunter, M. (1982). *Mastery teaching.* El Segundo, CA: TIP Publications.

Idol, L., & Jones, B. F. (Eds.). (1991). *Educational values and cognitive instruction: Implications for reform.* Mahwah, NJ: Erlbaum.

Irwin, J., LaGory, M., Ritchey, F., & Fitzpatrick, K. (2008). Social assets and mental distress among the homeless: Exploring the roles of social support and other forms of social capital on depression. *Social Science and Medicine, 67*(12), 1935–1943.

Jaser, S. S., Fear, J. M., Reeslund, K. L., Champion, J. E., Reising, M. M., & Compas, B. E. (2008). Maternal sadness and adolescents' responses to stress in offspring of mothers with and without a history of depression. *Journal of Clinical Child and Adolescent Psychology, 37*(4), 736–746.

Jensen, E. (1994). *The learning brain.* Del Mar, CA: Turning Point.

Jimenez, L., Dekovic, M., & Hidalgo, V. (in press). Adjustment of school-aged children and adolescents growing up in at-risk families: Relationships between family variables and individual, relational and school adjustment. *Children and Youth Services Review.*

Johnson, L. S. (2008). Relationship of instructional methods to student engagement in two public high schools. *American Secondary Education, 36*(2), 69–87.

Jones, B. F., Pierce, J., & Hunter, B. (1988). Teaching students to construct graphic representations. *Educational Leadership, 46*(4), 20–25.

Joos, M. (1967). The styles of the five clocks. In R. D. Abraham & R. C. Troike (Eds.), *Language and cultural diversity in American education* (pp. 145–149). Englewood Cliffs, NJ: Prentice Hall.

Jordan, H., Mendro, R., & Weerasinghe, D. (1997, July). *Teacher effects on longitudinal student achievement: A report on research in progress.* Retrieved June 16, 2009, from http://www.dallasisd.org/inside_disd/depts/evalacct/research/articles/Jordan-Teacher-Effects-on-Longitudinal-Student-Achievement-1997.pdf

Joshi, R. M. (2005). Vocabulary: A critical component of comprehension. *Reading and Writing Quarterly, 21*(3), 209–219.

Joyce, B., & Showers, B. (1988). Student achievement through staff development. New York: Longman.

Joyce, B., & Weil, M. (1986). *Models of teaching* (3rd ed.). Boston: Allyn & Bacon.

Kahlenberg, R. D. (2008). *Can separate be equal? The overlooked flaw at the center of No Child Left Behind: Updated for 2008.* Retrieved May 21, 2009, from http://www.tcf.org/Publications/Education/canseprev3.pdf

Kamps, D. M., Greenwood, C., Arreaga-Mayer, C., Veerkamp, M. B., Utley, C., Tapia, Y., et al. (2008). The efficacy of ClassWide Peer Tutoring in middle schools. *Education and Treatment of Children, 31*(2), 119–152.

Kashima, Y., Foddy, M., & Platow, M. (Eds.). (2002). *Self and identity: Personal, social and symbolic.* Mahwah, NJ: Erlbaum.

Kaylor, M., & Flores, M. M. (2007). Increasing academic motivation in culturally and linguistically diverse students from low socioeconomic backgrounds. *Journal of Advanced Academics, 19*(1), 66–89.

Kerpelman, J. L., Eryigit, S., & Stephens, C. J. (2008). African American adolescents' future education orientation: Associations with self-efficacy, ethnic identity, and perceived parental support. *Journal of Youth and Adolescence, 37*(8), 997–1008.

Kilpatrick, J., Swafford, J., & Findell, B. (Eds.). (2001). *Adding it up: Helping children learn mathematics.* Washington, DC: Mathematics Learning Study Committee, National Research Council.

King-Sears, M. E. (2008). Using teacher and researcher data to evaluate the effects of self-management in an inclusive classroom. *Preventing School Failure, 52*(4), 25–36.

Kinney, D. W. (2008). Selected demographic variables, school music participation, and achievement test scores of urban middle school students. *Journal of Research in Music Education, 56*(2), 145–161.

Kirby, N. F., & Downs, C. T. (2007). Assessment and the disadvantaged student: Potential for encouraging self-regulated learning? *Assessment and Evaluation in Higher Education, 32*(4), 475–494.

Kirkpatrick, L. C., & Klein, P. D. (2009). Planning text structure as a way to improve students' writing from sources in the compare-contrast genre. *Learning and Instruction, 19*(4), 309–321.

Kishiyama, M. M., Boyce, W. T., Jimenez, A. M., Perry, L. M., & Knight, R. T. (2009). Socioeconomic disparities affect prefrontal function in children. *Journal of Cognitive Neuroscience, 21*(6), 1106–1115.

Koch, L. M., Gross, A. M., & Kolts, R. (2001). Attitudes toward black English and code switching. *Journal of Black Psychology, 27*(1), 29–42.

Koegel, P., Melamid, E., & Burnam, M. A. (1995). Childhood risk factors of homelessness among homeless adults. *American Journal of Public Health, 85*(12), 1642–1649.

Kourea, L., Cartledge, G., & Musti-Rao, S. (2007). Improving the reading skills of urban elementary students through total class peer tutoring. *Remedial and Special Education, 28*(2), 95–107.

Krauss, S., Brunner, M., Kunter, M., Baumert, J., Neubrand, M., Blum, W., et al. (2008). Pedagogical content knowledge and content knowledge of secondary mathematics teachers. *Journal of Educational Psychology, 100*(3), 716–725.

Krebs, C. (2006). Using a dialogue journal to build responsibility and self-reliance: A case study. *RE:view, 37*(4), 173–176.

Krueger, K. A., & Dayan, P. (2009). Flexible shaping: How learning in small steps helps. *Cognition, 110*(3), 380–394.

Kunsch, C. A., Jitendra, A. K., & Sood, S. (2007). The effects of peer-mediated instruction in mathematics for students with learning problems: A research synthesis. *Learning Disabilities Research and Practice, 22*(1), 1–12.

Langford, P. A., Rizzo, S. K., & Roth, J. M. (2003). *Improving student comprehension in content areas through the use of reading strategies.* Unpublished master's thesis, Saint Xavier University, Chicago.

Latino high school youth in Indianapolis: The El Puente Project in retrospect: May 2001–June 2004. (2005). Retrieved October 2007 from http://www. elpuenteproject.com/defiles/3yearreport.pdf

Lave, J. (1988). *Cognition in practice: Mind, mathematics and culture in everyday life.* Cambridge, UK: Cambridge University Press.

Lave, J., & Wenger, E. (1991). *Situated learning: Legitimate peripheral participation.* Cambridge, UK: Cambridge University Press.

Leemkuil, H., Jong, T. D., & Ootes, S. (2000). *Review of educational use of games and simulations.* AE Enschede, Netherlands: University of Twente.

Leinhardt, G., & Greeno, J. G. (1991). The cognitive skill of teaching. In P. Goodyear (Ed.), *Teaching Knowledge and Intelligent Tutoring* (pp. 233–268). Norwood, NJ: Ablex.

Leondari, A. (2007). Future time perspective, possible selves, and academic achievement. *New Directions for Adult and Continuing Education, 114,* 17–26.

Lin, H., & Chen, T. (2006). Decreasing cognitive load for novice EFL learners: Effects of question and descriptive advance organizers in facilitating EFL learners' comprehension of an animation-based content lesson. *System, 34*(3), 416–431.

Littlewood, J. E. (1986). *Littlewood's miscellany.* Cambridge, UK: Cambridge University Press.

Lloyd, J. E. V., & Hertzman, C. (2009). From kindergarten readiness to fourth-grade assessment: Longitudinal analysis with linked population data. *Social Science and Medicine, 68*(1), 111–123.

Lodewyk, K. R., Winne, P. H., & Jamieson-Noel, D. L. (2009). Implications of task structure on self-regulated learning and achievement. *Educational Psychology, 29*(1), 1–25.

Louv, R. (2006). *The cradle of prosperity: Raising the new American economy.* Cambridge, MA: National Scientific Council on the Developing Child.

Lujan, M. L. (2006). *Critical thinking.* Tyler, TX: Mentoring Minds.

Maguire, E. A., Frith, C. D., & Morris, R. G. (1999). The functional neuroanatomy of comprehension and memory: The importance of prior knowledge. *Brain, 122*(10), 1839–1850.

Mahalingam, M., Schaefer, F., & Morlino, E. (2008). Promoting student learning through group problem solving in general chemistry recitations. *Journal of Chemical Education, 85*(11), 1577–1581.

Malewski, E., & Phillion, J. (2009). International field experiences: The impact of class, gender and race on the perceptions and experiences of preservice teachers. *Teaching and Teacher Education, 25*(1), 52–60.

Malka, A., & Covington, M. V. (2005). Perceiving school performance as instrumental to future goal attainment: Effects on graded performance. *Contemporary Educational Psychology, 30*(1), 60–80.

Malmberg, L.-E., Ehrman, J., & Lithen, T. (2005). Adolescents' and parents' future beliefs. *Journal of Adolescence, 28*(6), 709–723.

Manfra, L., & Winsler, A. (2006). Preschool children's awareness of private speech. *International Journal of Behavioral Development, 30*(6), 537–549.

Marzano, R. J. (2007). *The art and science of teaching: A comprehensive framework for effective instruction.* Alexandria, VA: Association for Supervision and Curriculum Development.

Marzano, R. J., & Arredondo, D. (1986). *Tactics for thinking.* Aurora, CO: Mid-Continent Regional Educational Laboratory.

Marzano, R. J., Pickering, D. J., & Pollock, J. E. (2001). *Classroom instruction that works: Research-based strategies for increasing student achievement.* Alexandria, VA: Association for Supervision and Curriculum Development.

Mason, L. H., & Shriner, J. G. (2008). Self-regulated strategy development instruction for writing an opinion essay: Effects for six students with emotional/behavior disorders. *Reading and Writing, 21*(1), 71–93.

Mattox, K., Hancock, D., & Queen, J. A. (2005). The effect of block scheduling on middle school students' mathematics achievement. *NASSP Bulletin, 89*(642), 3–13.

McCarthy, B. (1996). *About learning.* Barrington, IL: Excel.

McCrudden, M. T., Schraw, G., & Lehman, S. (2009). The use of adjunct displays to facilitate comprehension of causal relationships in expository text. *Instructional Science, 37*(1), 65–86.

McIntosh, K., Campbell, A. L., Carter, D. R., & Dickey, C. R. (2009). Differential effects of a tier two behavior intervention based on function of problem behavior. *Journal of Positive Behavior Interventions, 11*(2), 82–93.

McManus, D. O., Dunn, R., & Denig, S. J. (2003). Effects of traditional lecture versus teacher-constructed and student-constructed self-teaching instructional resources on short-term science achievement and attitudes. *American Biology Teacher, 65*(2), 93–102.

McTighe, J., & Lyman, F. T., Jr. (1988). Cueing thinking in the classroom: The promise of theory-embedded tools. *Educational Leadership, 45*(7), 18–24.

McWhorter, J. (2000). *Losing the race: Self-sabotage in black America.* New York: Harper Perennial.

Mental models for English/language arts: Grades 6–12. (2007). Highlands, TX: aha! Process.

Mental models for math: Grades 6–12. (2006). Highlands, TX: aha! Process.

Meyer, B. J. F., & Poon, L. W. (2001). Effects of structure strategy training and signaling on recall of text. *Journal of Educational Psychology, 93*(1), 141–159.

Miller, S. C. (2007). *Until it's gone: Ending poverty in our nation, in our lifetime.* Highlands, TX: aha! Process.

Milliken, B. (2007). *The last dropout: Stop the epidemic.* Carlsbad, CA: Hay House.

Mills, A. (1999). Pollyanna and the not so glad game. *Children's Literature, 27,* 87–104.

Mithaug, D. K. (2002). 'Yes' means success: Teaching children with multiple disabilities to self-regulate during independent work. *Teaching Exceptional Children, 35*(1), 22–27.

Mohan, B., & Slater, T. (2006). Examining the theory/practice relation in a high school science register: A functional linguistic perspective. *Journal of English for Academic Purposes, 5*(4), 302–316.

Montano-Harmon, M. R. (1991). Discourse features of written Mexican Spanish: Current research in contrastive rhetoric and its implications. *Hispania, 74*(2), 417–425.

Montelongo, J., Berber-Jimenez, L., Hernandez, A. C., & Hosking, D. (2006). Teaching expository text structures. *Science Teacher, 73*(2), 28–31.

Moore, D. W., Prebble, S., Robertson, J., Waetford, R., & Anderson, A. (2001). Self-recording with goal setting: A self-management programme for the classroom. *Educational Psychology, 21*(3), 255–265.

Morrison, J. A., & Young, T. A. (2008). Using science trade books to support inquiry in the elementary classroom. *Childhood Education, 84*(4), 204–208.

Najman, J. M., Aird, R., Bor, W., O'Callaghan, M., Williams, G. M., & Shuttlewood G. J. (2004). The generational transmission of socioeconomic inequalities in child cognitive development and emotional health. *Social Science and Medicine, 58*(6), 1147–1158.

Najman, J. M., Hayatbakhsh, M. R., Heron, M. A., Bor, W., O'Callaghan, M. J., & Williams, G. M. (2009). The impact of episodic and chronic poverty on child cognitive development. *The Journal of Pediatrics, 154*(2), 284–289.

Nam, Y., & Huang, J. (2009). Equal opportunity for all? Parental economic resources and children's educational attainment. *Children and Youth Services Review, 31*(6), 625–634.

National Institute of Child Health and Human Development. (2000). *Report of the National Reading Panel. Teaching children to read: An evidence-based assessment of the scientific research literature on reading and its implications for reading instruction* (NIH Publication No. 00–4769). Washington, DC: U.S. Government Printing Office.

Nelson, M. (2000). A case of preservice elementary teachers exploring, retelling, and reframing. *Research in Science Education, 30*(4), 417–433.

Ngu, B. H., Mit, E., Shahbodin, F., & Tuovinen, J. (2009). Chemistry problem solving instruction: A comparison of three computer-based formats for learning from hierarchical network problem representations. *Instructional Science, 37*(1), 21–42.

O'Dell, C., & Grayson, J. C., Jr., with Essaides, N. (1998). *If only we knew what we know.* New York: Free Press.

Olmedo, I. M. (2009). Blending borders of language and culture: Schooling in La Villita. *Journal of Latinos and Education, 8*(1), 22–37.

Oshry, B. (1995). *Seeing systems: Unlocking the mysteries of organizational life.* San Francisco: Berrett-Koehler.

Ostad, S. A., & Askeland, M. (2008). Sound-based number facts training in a private speech internalization perspective: Evidence for effectiveness of an intervention in grade 3. *Journal of Research in Childhood Education, 23*(1), 109–124.

Palincsar, A. S., & Brown, A. L. (1984). The reciprocal teaching of comprehension-fostering and comprehension-monitoring activities. *Cognition and Instruction, 1*(2), 117–175.

Paquette, K. R., Fello, S. E., & Jalongo, M. R. (2007). The talking drawings strategy: Using primary children's illustrations and oral language to improve comprehension of expository text. *Early Childhood Education Journal, 35*(1), 65–73.

Parker, M., & Hurry, J. (2007). Teachers' use of questioning and modeling comprehension skills in primary classrooms. *Educational Review, 59*(3), 299–314.

Pasley, K., Furtis, T. G., & Skinner, M. L. (2002). Effects of commitment and psychological centrality on fathering. *Journal of Marriage and Family, 64*(1), 130–138.

Payne, R. K. (1996). *A framework for understanding and working with students and adults from poverty.* Baytown, TX: RFT.

Payne, R. K. (2002). *Understanding learning: The how, the why, the what.* Highlands, TX: aha! Process.

Payne, R. K. (2005a). *A framework for understanding poverty* (5th ed.). Highlands, TX: aha! Process.

Payne, R. K. (2005b). *Learning structures* (4th ed.). Highlands, TX: aha! Process.

Payne, R. K. (2006). *Working with parents: Building relationships for student success.* Highlands, TX: aha! Process.

Payne, R. K., DeVol, P. E., & Smith, T. D. (2006). *Bridges out of poverty: Strategies for professionals and communities* (4th ed.). Highlands, TX: aha! Process.

Payne, R. K., & Krabill, D. L. (2002). *Hidden rules of class at work.* Highlands, TX: aha! Process.

Payne, R. K., & Magee, D. S. (2001). *Meeting standards & raising test scores—When you don't have much time or money.* Highlands, TX: aha! Process.

Peer tutoring and response groups: What Works Clearinghouse intervention report. (2007). Princeton, NJ: What Works Clearinghouse. (ERIC Document Reproduction Service No. ED499296)

Petermann, F., & Natzke, H. (2008). Preliminary results of a comprehensive approach to prevent antisocial behaviour in preschool and primary school pupils in Luxembourg. *School Psychology International, 29*(5), 606–626.

Peters, G. (2002). *Perceptions of principals and teachers regarding frames used in decision-making.* Unpublished dissertation, University of Alabama.

Peterson, L. D., Young, K., Richard, S., Charles, L., West, R. P., & Hill, M. (2006). Using self-management procedures to improve classroom social skills in multiple general education settings. *Education and Treatment of Children, 29*(1), 1–21.

Phalet, K., Andriessen, I., & Lens, W. (2004). How future goals enhance motivation and learning in multicultural classrooms. *Educational Psychology Review, 16*(1), 59–89.

Piro, J. M., & Ortiz, C. (2009). The effect of piano lessons on the vocabulary and verbal sequencing skills of primary grade students. *Psychology of Music.* DOI: 10.1177/0305735608097248

Pitner, R. O., & Astor, R. A. (2008). Children's reasoning about poverty, physical deterioration, danger, and retribution in neighborhood contexts. *Journal of Environmental Psychology, 28*(4), 327–338.

Porter, A. C., & Brophy, J. (1988). Synthesis of research on good teaching: Insights from the work of the Institute for Research on Teaching. *Educational Leadership, 45*(8), 74–85.

Po-ying, C. (2007). How students react to the power and responsibility of being decision makers in their own learning. *Language Teaching Research, 11*(2), 225–241.

Prisoners of time. (1994). Report of the National Education Commission on Teaching and Learning. Retrieved May 21, 2009, from http://www.ed.gov/pubs/ PrisonersOfTime/index.html

Putnam, R. D. (2000). *Bowling alone: The collapse and revival of American community.* New York: Simon & Schuster.

Rafferty, Y., & Shinn, M. (1991). The impact of homelessness on children. *American Psychologist, 46*(11), 1170–1179.

Rapee, R. M., Gaston, J. E., & Abbott, M. J. (2009). Testing the efficacy of theoretically derived improvements in the treatment of social phobia. *Journal of Consulting and Clinical Psychology, 77*(2), 317–327.

Ratey, J., & Hageman, E. (2008). *Spark: The revolutionary new science of exercise and the brain.* New York: Little, Brown.

Rauscher, F. H. (1999). Music exposure and the development of spatial intelligence in children. *Bulletin of the Council for Research in Music Education, 142,* 35–47.

Razumnikova, O. M. (2005). The interaction between gender stereotypes and life values as factors in the choice of profession. *Russian Education and Society, 47*(12), 21–33.

Reddy, L. A., De Thomas, C. A., Newman, E., & Chun, V. (2009). School-based prevention and intervention programs for children with emotional disturbance: A review of treatment components and methodology. *Psychology in the Schools, 46*(2), 132–153.

Reiner, M. (2009). Sensory cues, visualization and physics learning. International *Journal of Science Education, 31*(3), 343–364.

Reis, S. M., Colbert, R. D., & Hebert, T. P. (2005). Understanding resilience in diverse, talented students in an urban high school. *Roeper Review, 27*(2), 110.

Resnick, L. B., & Klopfer, L. (Eds.). (1989). *Toward the thinking curriculum: Current cognitive research.* Alexandria, VA: Association for Supervision and Curriculum Development.

Richards, A. G. (2003). Arts and academic achievement in reading: Functions and implications. *Art Education, 56*(6), 19–23.

Richards, J. C., & Anderson, N. A. (2003). How do you know? A strategy to help emergent readers make inferences. *Reading Teacher, 57*(3), 290–293.

Ridley, M. (2000). *Genome: The autobiography of a species in 23 chapters.* New York: HarperCollins.

Rieber, L. P. (2005). Multimedia learning in games, simulations, and microworlds. In R. E. Mayer (Ed.), *The Cambridge handbook of multimedia learning* (pp. 549–567). Cambridge, UK: Cambridge University Press.

Rieber, R. W. (Ed.). (1997). *The collected works of L. S. Vygotsky: Vol. 4. The history of the development of higher mental functions.* New York: Plenum Press.

Riley, L. P., LaMontagne, L. L., Hepworth, J. T., & Murphy, B. A. (2007). Parental grief responses and personal growth following the death of a child. *Death Studies, 31*(4), 277–299.

Rimm-Kaufman, S. E., & Chiu, Y.-J. I. (2007). Promoting social and academic competence in the classroom: An intervention study examining the contribution of the 'responsive classroom' approach. *Psychology in the Schools, 44*(4), 397–413.

Robbins, R. N., & Bryan, A. (2004). Relationships between future orientation, impulsive sensation seeking, and risk behavior among adjudicated adolescents. *Journal of Adolescent Research, 19*(4), 428–445.

Rocha, E. (2008). *Expanded learning time in action: Initiatives in high-poverty and high-minority schools and districts.* Retrieved May 21, 2009, from http://www.americanprogress.org/issues/2008/07/elt_report1.html

Rogevich, M. E., & Perin, D. (2008). Effects on science summarization of a reading comprehension intervention for adolescents with behavior and attention disorders. *Exceptional Children, 74*(2), 135–154.

Rohrer, T. (2006). Image schemata in the brain. In B. Hampe (Ed.), *From perception to meaning: Image schemas in cognitive linguistics* (pp. 165–198). Berlin: Mouton de Gruyter.

Roscoe, R. D., & Chi, M. T. H. (2008). Tutor learning: The role of explaining and responding to questions. *Instructional Science, 36*(4), 321–350.

Rosenholtz, S. J. (1989). *Teachers' workplace: The social organization of schools.* New York: Longman.

Ross, D. D., Bondy, E., Gallingane, C., & Hambacher, E. (2008). Promoting academic engagement through insistence: Being a warm demander. *Childhood Education, 84*(3), 142–146.

Ross, J. A., & Starling, M. (2008). Self-assessment in a technology-supported environment: The case of grade 9 geography. *Assessment in Education, 15*(2), 183–199.

Ryken, A. E. (2006). Goin' somewhere: How career technical education programs support and constrain urban youths' career decision-making. *Career and Technical Education Research, 31*(1), 49–71.

Sanchez, B., Reyes, O., & Singh, J. (2006). Makin' it in college: The value of significant individuals in the lives of Mexican American adolescents. *Journal of Hispanic Higher Education, 5*(1), 48–67.

Sanders, W. L., & Rivers, J. C. (1996). Cumulative and residual effects of teachers on future student academic achievement. Retrieved May 21, 2009, from http://www.mccsc.edu/~curriculum/cumulative%20and%20residual%20effects%20of%20teachers.pdf

Sapolsky, R. M. (1998). *Why zebras don't get ulcers.* New York: W. H. Freeman.

Scales, P. C., Benson, P. L., Roehlkepartain, E. C., Sesma, A., Jr., & van Dulmen, M. (2006). The role of developmental assets in predicting academic achievement: A longitudinal study. *Journal of Adolescence, 29*(5), 691–708.

Schacter, J. (2001). Reading programs that work: An evaluation of kindergarten-through-third-grade reading instructional programs. *ERS Spectrum, 19*(4), 12–25.

Schamberg, M. (2008). The cost of living in poverty: Long-term effects of allostatic load on working memory. Retrieved May 21, 2009, from http://ecommons.library.cornell.edu/bitstream/1813/10814/1/Schamberg%20-%20Pov%2c%20Load%2c%20Working%20Mem.pdf

Schellenberg, R. C., Parks-Savage, A., & Rehfuss, M. (2007). Reducing levels of elementary school violence with peer mediation. *Professional School Counseling, 10*(5), 475–481.

Scherff, L., & Singer, N. R. (2008). Framing and re-framing through computer-mediated communication: Providing pre-service teachers with alternate support structures. *Learning Inquiry, 2*(3), 151–167.

Schnotz, W., & Kurschner, C. (2008). External and internal representations in the acquisition and use of knowledge: Visualization effects on mental model construction. *Instructional Science, 36*(3), 175–190.

Schraw, G., Brooks, D., & Crippen, K. J. (2005). Using an interactive, compensatory model of learning to improve chemistry teaching. *Journal of Chemical Education, 82*(4), 637–640.

Seebaum, M. (1999). *A picture is worth a thousand words.* Highlands, TX: aha! Process.

Seginer, R. (2008). Future orientation in times of threat and challenge: How resilient adolescents construct their future. *International Journal of Behavioral Development, 32*(4), 272–282.

Seligman, M. (2002). *Authentic happiness.* New York: Free Press.

Senge, P., McCabe, N. H. C., Lucas, T., Kleiner, A., Dutton, J., & Smith, B. (2000). *Schools that learn: A fifth discipline fieldbook for educators, parents, and everyone who cares about education.* New York: Broadway Business.

Senge, P., Ross, R., Smith, B., Roberts, C., & Kleiner, A. (1994). *The fifth discipline fieldbook: Strategies and tools for building a learning organization.* New York: Doubleday-Currency.

Shamir, A., & Lazerovitz, T. (2007). Peer mediation: Intervention for scaffolding self-regulated learning among children with learning disabilities. *European Journal of Special Needs Education, 22*(3), 255–273.

Shamir, A., Tzuriel, D., & Rozen, M. (2006). Peer mediation: The effects of program intervention, maths level, and verbal ability on mediation style and improvement in maths problem solving. *School Psychology International, 27*(2), 209–231.

Sharron, H., & Coulter, M. (2004). *Changing children's minds: Feuerstein's revolution in the teaching of intelligence.* Highlands, TX: aha! Process.

Shonkoff, J. P., & Phillips, D. A. (Eds.). (2000). *From neurons to neighborhoods: The science of early childhood development.* Washington, DC: National Academy Press.

Shulman, L. S. (1987). Assessment for teaching: An initiative for the profession. *Phi Delta Kappan, 69*(1), 38–44.

Shulman, L. S. (1988). A union of insufficiencies: Strategies for teacher assessment in a period of educational reform. *Educational Leadership, 46*(3), 36–41.

Sibley, B. A., Ward, R. M., Yazvac, T. S., Zullig, K., & Potteiger, J. A. (2008). Making the grade with diet and exercise. *AASA Journal of Scholarship and Practice, 5*(2), 38–45.

Simonsen, B., Fairbanks, S., Briesch, A., Myers, D., & Sugai, G. (2008). Evidence-based practices in classroom management: Considerations for research to practice. *Education and Treatment of Children, 31*(3), 351–380.

Singh, C. (2008). *Assessing student expertise in introductory physics with isomorphic problems. I. Performance on nonintuitive problem pair from introductory physics.* Retrieved May 20, 2009, from http://prst-per.aps.org/pdf/PRSTPER/v4/i1/e010104

Smith, C., Wiser, M., Anderson, C. & Krajcik, J. (2006). Implications of research on children's learning for standards and assessment: A proposed learning progression for matter and atomic-molecular theory. *Measurement, 14*(1&2), 1–98.

Souther, E. (2008a). *Facilitator guide for the R rules: A guide for teens to identify and build resources.* Highlands, TX: aha! Process.

Souther, E. (2008b). *The R rules: A guide for teens to identify and build resources.* Highlands, TX: aha! Process.

Southgate, D. E., & Roscigno, V. J. (2009). The impact of music on childhood and adolescent achievement. *Social Science Quarterly, 90*(1), 4–21.

Stamou, E., Theodorakis, Y., Kokaridas, D., Perkos, S., & Kessanopoulou, M. (2007). The effect of self-talk on the penalty execution in goalball. *British Journal of Visual Impairment, 25*(3), 233–247.

Star, J. R., & Rittle-Johnson, B. (2008). Flexibility in problem solving: The case of equation solving. *Learning and Instruction, 18*(6), 565–579.

Steiner, C. (1994). *Scripts people live: Transactional analysis of life scripts.* New York: Grove Press.

Stewart, R. M., Benner, G. J., Martella, R. C., & Marchand-Martella, N. E. (2007). Three-tier models of reading and behavior: A research review. *Journal of Positive Behavior Interventions, 9*(4), 239–253.

Stewart, T. A. (1997). *Intellectual capital: The new wealth of organizations.* New York: Doubleday-Currency.

Stichter, J. P., Lewis, T. J., Whittaker, T. A., Richter, M., Johnson, N. W., & Trussell, R. P. (2009). Assessing teacher use of opportunities to respond and effective classroom management strategies: Comparisons among high- and low-risk elementary schools. *Journal of Positive Behavior Interventions, 11*(2), 68–81.

Stoeger, H., & Ziegler, A. (2008). Evaluation of a classroom based training to improve self-regulation in time management tasks during homework activities with fourth graders. *Metacognition and Learning, 3*(3), 207–230.

Stone, R. H., Boon, R. T., Fore, C., III, Bender, W. N., & Spencer, V. G. (2008). Use of text maps to improve the reading comprehension skills among students in high school with emotional and behavioral disorders. *Behavioral Disorders, 33*(2), 87–98.

Success stories/evidence data. (2006). Retrieved May 21, 2009, from http://www.projectread.com/success-stories-evidence-data-con-20.html

Sullivan, F. R. (2008). Robotics and science literacy: Thinking skills, science process skills and systems understanding. *Journal of Research in Science Teaching, 45*(3), 373–394.

Sveiby, K. E. (1997). *The new organizational wealth: Managing and measuring knowledge-based assets.* San Francisco: Berrett-Koehler.

Swan, K., van't Hooft, M., Kratcoski, A., & Unger, D. (2005). Uses and effects of mobile computing devices in K–8 classrooms. *Journal of Research on Technology in Education, 38*(1), 99–112.

Tabachnick, S. E., Miller, R. B., & Relyea, G. E. (2008). The relationships among students' future-oriented goals and subgoals, perceived task instrumentality, and task-oriented self-regulation strategies in an academic environment. *Journal of Educational Psychology, 100*(3), 629–642.

Tanenhaus, M. K., Spivey-Knowlton, M. J., Eberhard, K. M., & Sedivy, J. C. (1995). Integration of visual and linguistic information in spoken language comprehension. *Science, 268*(5217), 1632–1634.

Texas administrative code, title 19, part II, chapter 112. Texas essential knowledge and skills for science. (n.d.). Retrieved June 11, 2009, from http://ritter.tea.state.tx.us/rules/tac/chapter112/index.html

Thompson, D. D., & McDonald, D. M. (2007). Examining the influence of teacher-constructed and student-constructed assignments on the achievement patterns of gifted and advanced sixth-grade students. *Journal for the Education of the Gifted, 31*(2), 198–226.

Thompson, R. L., Vinson, D. P., & Vigliocco, G. (2009). The link between form and meaning in American Sign Language: Lexical processing effects. *Journal of Experimental Psychology, 35*(2), 550–557.

Tomporowski, P. D., Davis, C. L., Miller, P. H., & Naglieri, J. A. (2008). Exercise and children's intelligence, cognition, and academic achievement. *Educational Psychology Review, 20*(2), 111–131.

Traore, R. (2008). Cultural connections: An alternative to conflict resolution. *Multicultural Education, 15*(4), 10–14.

Tremarche, P. V., Robinson, E. M., & Graham, L. B. (2007). Physical education and its effect on elementary testing results. *Physical Educator, 64*(2), 58–64.

Tucker, B. H. (2005). *The journey of Al and Gebra to the land of algebra.* Highlands, TX: aha! Process.

Tucker, B. H. (2007). *Reading by age 5.* Highlands, TX: aha! Process.

Tzuriel, D., & Shamir, A. (2007). The effects of peer mediation with young children (PMYC) on children's cognitive modifiability. *British Journal of Educational Psychology, 77*(1), 143–165.

Ury, W., Fisher, R., & Patton, B. (1991). *Getting to yes: Negotiating an agreement without giving in* (2nd ed.). Boston: Houghton Mifflin Harcourt.

van den Bos, K. P., Nakken, H., Nicolay, P. G., & van Houten, E. J. (2007). Adults with mild intellectual disabilities: Can their reading comprehension ability be improved? *Journal of Intellectual Disability Research, 51*(11), 835–849.

van der Schoot, M., Vasbinder, A. L., Horsley, T. M., & van Lieshout, E. C. D. M. (2008). The role of two reading strategies in text comprehension: An eye fixation study in primary school children. *Journal of Research in Reading, 31*(2), 203–223.

Van Meter, P., Aleksic, M., Schwartz, A., & Garner, J. (2006). Learner-generated drawing as a strategy for learning from content area text. *Contemporary Educational Psychology, 31*(2), 142–166.

Veerkamp, M. B., Kamps, D. M., & Cooper, L. (2007). The effects of ClassWide Peer Tutoring on the reading achievement of urban middle school students. *Education and Treatment of Children, 30*(2), 21–51.

Vestal, A., & Jones, N. A. (2004). Peace building and conflict resolution in preschool children. *Journal of Research in Childhood Education, 19*(2), 131.

Vickerstaff, S., Heriot, S., Wong, M., Lopes, A., & Dossetor, D. (2007). Intellectual ability, self-perceived social competence, and depressive symptomatology in children with high-functioning autistic spectrum disorders. *Journal of Autism and Developmental Disorders, 37*(9), 1647–1664.

Wagner, T. (2008). *The global achievement gap.* New York: Basic Books.

Walberg, H. J. (1990). Productive teaching and instruction: Assessing the knowledge base. *Phi Delta Kappan, 71*(6), 470–478.

Waring, T. M. (in press). New evolutionary foundations: Theoretical requirements for a science of sustainability. *Ecological Economics.*

Watson, B., & Konicek, R. (1990). Teaching for conceptual change: Confronting children's experience. *Phi Delta Kappan, 71*(9), 680–685.

Watson, S., & Miller, T. (2009). Classification and the dichotomous key: Tools for teaching identification. *Science Teacher, 76*(3), 50–54.

Weekes, H. (2005). Drawing students out: Using sketching exercises to hone observation skills. *Science Teacher, 72*(1), 34–37.

Wenger, E. (1999). *Communities of practice: Learning, meaning, and identity.* Cambridge, UK: Cambridge University Press.

Whalon, K., & Hanline, M. F. (2008). Effects of a reciprocal questioning intervention on the question generation and responding of children with autism spectrum disorder. *Education and Training in Developmental Disabilities, 43*(3), 367–387.

What research says about parent involvement in children's education in relation to academic achievement. (2002). Retrieved May 19, 2009, from http://www.michigan.gov/documents/Final_Parent_Involvement_Fact_Sheet_14732_7.pdf

Wheeler, R. S. (2008). Becoming adept at code-switching. *Educational Leadership, 65*(7), 54–58.

Wiggins, G., & McTighe, J. (1998). *Understanding by design.* Alexandria, VA: Association for Supervision and Curriculum Development.

Williams, A., Rouse, K., Seals, C., & Gilbert, J. (2009). Enhancing reading literacy in elementary children using programming for scientific simulations. *International Journal on E-Learning, 8*(1), 57–69.

Williams, J. P. (2005). Instruction in reading comprehension for primary-grade students: 'A focus on text structure.' *Journal of Special Education, 39*(1), 6–18.

Williams, J. P., Hall, K. M., & Lauer, K. D. (2004). Teaching expository text structure to young at-risk learners: Building the basics of comprehension instruction. *Exceptionality, 12*(3), 129–144.

Williams, J. P., Hall, K. M., Lauer, K. D., Stafford, K. B., DeSisto, L. A., & deCani, J. S. (2005). Expository text comprehension in the primary grade classroom. *Journal of Educational Psychology, 97*(4), 538–550.

Williams, J. P., Stafford, K. B., Lauer, K. D., Hall, K. M., & Pollini, S. (2009). Embedding reading comprehension training in content-area instruction. *Journal of Educational Psychology, 101*(1), 1–20.

Wilson, E. O. (1998). *Consilience: The unity of knowledge.* New York: Alfred A. Knopf.

Wise, A. (1995). *The high performance mind: Mastering brainwaves for insight, healing, and creativity.* New York: Tarcher/Putnam.

Wolff, J. (2002). *Proven practices: 'More time on task' benefits students at risk. In evidence: Policy reports from the CFE trial, Vol. 5.* New York: Campaign for Fiscal Equity. (ERIC Document Reproduction Service No. ED472576)

Wong, H. K., & Wong, R. T. (1998). *The first day of school: How to be an effective teacher* (Rev. ed.). Mountainview, CA: Author.

Woodward-Kron, R. (2008). More than just jargon: The nature and role of specialist language in learning disciplinary knowledge. *Journal of English for Academic Purposes, 7*(4), 234–249.

Wright, J. C., & Huston, A. C. (1995). *Effects of educational TV viewing of lower income preschoolers on academic skills, school readiness, and school adjustment one to three years later. A report to Children's Television Workshop.* Lawrence, KS: University of Kansas.

Yeung, W.-J. J., & Pfeiffer, K. M. (in press). The black-white test score gap and early home environment. *Social Science Research.*

You do the math: Explaining basic concepts behind math problems improves children's learning. (2009). Retrieved May 19, 2009, from http://www.sciencedaily.com/releases/2009/04/090410143809.htm

Yumusak, N., Sungur, S., & Cakiroglu, J. (2007). Turkish high school students' biology achievement in relation to academic self-regulation. *Educational Research and Evaluation, 13*(1), 53–69.

Ziesemer, C., Marcoux, L., & Marwell, B. E. (1994). Homeless children: Are they different from other low-income children? *Social Work, 39*(6), 658–668.

Zima, B. T., Wells, K. B., & Freeman, H. (1994). Emotional and behavioral problems and severe academic delays among sheltered homeless children in Los Angeles County. *American Journal of Public Health, 84*(2), 260–264.

Zuckerman, E. L. (2005). *Clinician's thesaurus: The guide to conducting interviews and writing psychological reports* (6th ed.). New York: Guilford.

Zull, J. E. (2002). *The art of changing the brain: Enriching the practice of teaching by exploring the biology of learning.* Sterling, VA: Stylus.